George Clooney

Anatomy of an Actor

George Clooney

Jeremy Smith

Introduction

'He's very handsome.'
'He knows it.'
An episode of *E/R*

In 2003 the American Academy of Facial Plastic and Reconstructive Surgery declared George Clooney the 'male modern-day ideal face of beauty'.[1] Citing his 'strong jaw, deep brown eyes, an ever-perfect olive complexion, and a strong and straight masculine nose',[2] the Academy, perhaps departing from its area of expertise, also celebrated the actor's 'charming personality',[3] noting that his warm and mischievous nature placed a disarming topspin on his physical attractiveness. This was hardly the first time Clooney had been honoured for his genetic good fortune (he had already been named *People Magazine*'s Sexiest Man Alive, and would receive the honour again), but it was unique in its absurd attempt to quantify, with some scientific backing, why the world is so enamoured of the actor.

Solving the conundrum of George Clooney – that knockout cocktail of looks, smarts and charisma – is similar to divining the mystique of Clark Gable, Cary Grant or Paul Newman; though there is a fairly complete record of their evolution from awkward acting novice to self-possessed movie star, there is no accounting for the to-the-silver-screen-born presence that was evident even in their earliest outings. Some of these gentlemen got off to more confident starts than others, but even a miscast and visibly embarrassed Newman in *The Silver Chalice* (1954), his first feature role, exudes a galvanic allure. The performance may be wooden, but one's focus is constantly drawn to the handsome fellow struggling to make this stilted material sing – and it is not his well-proportioned facial skeleton or those penetrating blue eyes that wins one over, but rather the ineffable essence that is and always would be Paul Newman. There is no measurement for this. He was just *there*, and he was never less than sublime – even when he could not figure out why he was not any good in that particular film.

Clooney was just *there*, too, when he strutted through the sliding doors of an emergency room in the pilot episode of *E/R* – the short-lived 1984 CBS sitcom, *not* the NBC drama that would launch his career a decade later. Clad in a hideous blue jacket, cheap sunglasses and beige shirt that looks awful on him and, therefore, everyone in the history of humanity who ever wore one like it, Clooney ably goes through the motions as a sandwich-munching slob of an Emergency Medical Technician named 'Ace'. The character is a type, and the twenty-three-year-old Clooney is in sufficient command of his instrument to imbue the role with a gangly, goofball insouciance, but what stands out in the scene (aside from Clooney's unfortunate mullet) is that boundless confidence that would keep him working steadily throughout his twenties, even when the television shows kept failing and the movie parts kept underwhelming. As with Newman in *The Silver Chalice*, the question is not whether Clooney can act; it is simply a matter of finding a project that will fully and emphatically exploit what everyone knew from the moment he stepped in front of a camera. As former President and CEO of Warner Bros. Television Leslie Moonves put it: 'Even before *ER*, Warner Bros. had him under contract because we felt it was only a question of time before he popped and became a major television star. There is, with George, this match of personality and talent. A lot of times you get one or the other, not both. With George, what you see on-screen is what you see off-screen. He can be a huge movie star.'[4] The only person who ever seriously doubted this potential was Clooney's father.

The Throwback

George Timothy Clooney was born to Nick Clooney and Nina Warren in Lexington, Kentucky, on 6 May 1961. Nick was a well-known regional broadcaster and brother of the then popular cabaret singer Rosemary Clooney, and his close proximity to the entertainment industry ensured a shortcut of sorts for his son, provided there was a predilection in any manner towards the discipline. The elder Clooney's television endeavours throughout the 1960s were something of a family affair, benefiting from the on and off-camera contributions of Nina, their eldest child, Adelia, and young George. It was this inclusive, down-to-earth quality that won over Midwestern viewers when they switched on *The Nick Clooney Show* (briefly broadcast in Columbus, Ohio, before moving

Top: Betty Clooney, Rosemary Clooney, Nick Clooney at home, 1958.

Bottom: Elliott Gould, Conchata Ferrell, George Clooney and Mary McDonnell in *E/R* (1984–5), the short-lived CBS sitcom, not the NBC drama that would launch his career a decade later.

to Cincinnati for several years). When Nick would interview his children for a cute segment, people were inviting the entire Clooney clan into their living rooms. This is the intimacy that still sets television apart from film, and it is precisely this quality that established the Clooneys as a largely beloved brood in Southwest Ohio and Northern Kentucky – the 'largely' qualifier being necessary due to Nick's unflagging commitment to the Democratic Party in an area where politics is a savagely divisive blood sport (as Nick would witness firsthand in 2004 when he waged an unsuccessful campaign for a seat in the US House of Representatives).

The Clooneys' political convictions grew out of a deep sense of social justice instilled primarily by their strict Catholic upbringing; they believed strongly in aiding the unfortunate and standing up for the oppressed. 'On Christmas morning,' recalled Clooney, 'before we could open our Christmas presents, we would go to this stranger's home and bring them presents. I remember helping clean the house up and putting up a tree. My father believed that you have a responsibility to look after everyone else.'[5] When it came to exacting justice for a perceived wrong, Nick Clooney observes that his son's ferocity was seemingly built-in. 'George had a kind of a sense of irony and justice from the very beginning', he remembers. 'When he was very, very little – maybe three – we were at his grandparents, and there was a puppy there. He was playing with the puppy and the puppy snapped at him. That was the first time that had ever happened to him, and he was outraged. And he cried, but he also picked the puppy up and bit it. What a perfect sense of justice. The puppy was just as outraged as he was.'[6] This penchant for physical altercations would remain undiminished throughout Clooney's life; he never backed down from a fistfight with a rural bigot, and there is, of course, his infamous scuffle with filmmaker David O. Russell on the set of *Three Kings* (1999), which was allegedly prompted by the director's mistreatment of extras.

That strict Catholic upbringing encouraged a mild degree of rebellion during Clooney's high-school years, but the wild behaviour did not commence until he was out of the house and on his own at Northern Kentucky University, were he failed to obtain a degree in Broadcast Journalism. He briefly transferred to the University of Cincinnati, where he succumbed to the narcotic excess of the fading disco era. 'All the designer drugs were okay', recalls Clooney. 'Quaaludes and blow. So that was the time in college for me: drugs and chasing girls. I came from a town of 1,500 people to Cincinnati. I would visit class every once in a while and stop by and go, "How's everybody doing?" I was still a responsible kid, but I didn't take school seriously. I had jobs. I sold women's suits and shoes and worked in

stockrooms of department stores, and I cut tobacco when it was the season. I was paying for my thing along the way.'[7] But school quickly lost whatever attraction it held for Clooney. This scholastic indifference coincided with Clooney's cousin Miguel Ferrer arriving in Kentucky to shoot a horse racing comedy called *And They Are Off* (1982) with his father, José Ferrer (Clooney's uncle by marriage to his Aunt Rosemary). Though the film was never finished, Clooney did manage some time on set as an extra, which led Miguel to suggest that his handsome cousin might consider moving to Hollywood to try his hand at acting. Being a college dropout with only a few hundred dollars to his name, Clooney thought this was a fine idea. His father, however, disagreed. 'I was saying how silly that was', recalled the elder Clooney. 'What a dumb idea for him to be an actor. I said, "George, let's look at the numbers. How many people are making a real living as an actor right now in the world? In the United States, maybe 5,000?" I said there are probably 50,000 of us making a living in broadcasting. So I was pushing him hard. Of course, the moral of this story is: always listen to your father.'[8] Clooney did not, and, at the age of twenty-one, he turned up at his Aunt Rosemary's Beverly Hills mansion in a rusted-out 1976 Monte Carlo.

The Cathode Ray Crucible

Clooney earned his Screen Actors Guild card soon after arriving in Los Angeles ('I played a bad guy [on *Riptide*], holding three girls hostage'[9]), thus granting him entry to a variety of marginal television roles that are memorable only for being so shockingly unworthy of his skills. He was still a few years away from being dubbed 'The Next Cary Grant' when he wandered seemingly undirected onto the burned-down 'Edna's Edibles' set of *The Facts of Life* in 1985. The NBC sitcom was in its seventh season and begging for the glue factory at the moment Clooney made his début as George Burnett, a local construction worker with two character quirks: he reads the *Kuwait Times* and likes to have fun. Adding Clooney to such a banal, sexless show was a humdrum harbinger for the rest of his 1980s and early '90s television run: producers and casting agents desperately wanted to be the ones to 'discover' Clooney, but they just did not have the material. And when Clooney did happen to find his way onto a pop cultural juggernaut in its maiden season, the creative brain trust of *Roseanne* wrote him out of the show. (Not that anyone was terribly worried about his future. 'Even then I could tell he had a bigger agenda', remembers co-star John Goodman.[10]) It is difficult to sympathize with a human being as gifted in every conceivable way as Clooney, but watching the enormously talented actor slog his way through the 1991 pilot episode of *Baby Talk*, an ABC sitcom based on Amy Heckerling's

surprise blockbuster *Look Who's Talking*, was excruciating. Cast again as a lovable lout of a construction worker, Clooney gave the show the effort it deserved – which is to say he looked sharp and memorized his lines. Mostly, though, he looked like he wanted to be anywhere else. There is a lethargy to his *Baby Talk* performance; it is the quiet exasperation of an actor desperate to inhabit a character rather than coast on his genetic code.

Almost a decade after rolling up on Aunt Rosemary's driveway, Clooney had been typecast as a reasonably articulate beefcake; he had blown past thirty years of age, and was best known for being the outlandishly attractive guy on shows speeding toward cancellation. 'In the way I was raised,' says Clooney, 'this is the time when you make your mark. In your twenties, you figure out what it is you're going to be. You do a lot of different jobs. By your late twenties, you sort of have some idea of what that is. Then you spend your thirties and a lot of your forties making your mark.'[11]

The Mark

'I fought to get *ER* and I got it and it changed my life', says Clooney, dramatically understating the impact the groundbreaking NBC medical drama had on his career.[12] Clooney was just a vaguely familiar face to avid television viewers

before the pilot episode of *ER* aired on 19 September 1994; after that night, he *was* Dr. Doug Ross, the brilliant, compassionate, devastatingly handsome paediatrics resident whose sexual appetite is matched only by his hunger for social justice. Though Ross's bushy hair was a peculiar choice early on (if a model of restraint compared to Clooney's decade-long commitment to the mullet), the producers quickly settled on a classic Caesar haircut that let the actor's visage and personality do the seducing. Viewers fell hard and quickly. 'The product you're selling out there is you', says Clooney. 'It's not like, "Here's another set of encyclopedias if you don't like this one."'[13] This was the major A-list break Clooney had been chasing since he drove cross country from Augusta, Kentucky, in 1982, and he was humble enough to observe that his pragmatic nature probably had more to do with his break-through than any innate acting skill. 'When you've failed enough,' says Clooney, 'you learn how to be better at the business. I'm probably better at the business side than I am at acting.'[14]

Self-deprecation is another charming Clooney trait. It is as if he is apologizing for the inevitability of his stardom, pleading the world's forgiveness for their involuntary affection. He cannot help that he is the man others would like to be or be with. 'Yes, he's funny as hell', explains Cate Blanchett, his co-star in *The Good German* (2006) and *The Monuments Men* (2014).

Above: Mindy Cohn, Nancy McKeon and George Clooney in *The Facts of Life* (1979–88).

Opposite: Cast as Dr. Doug Ross in *ER* (1994–2009), Clooney is the breakout star of a show that immediately becomes the second-highest-rated show on television.

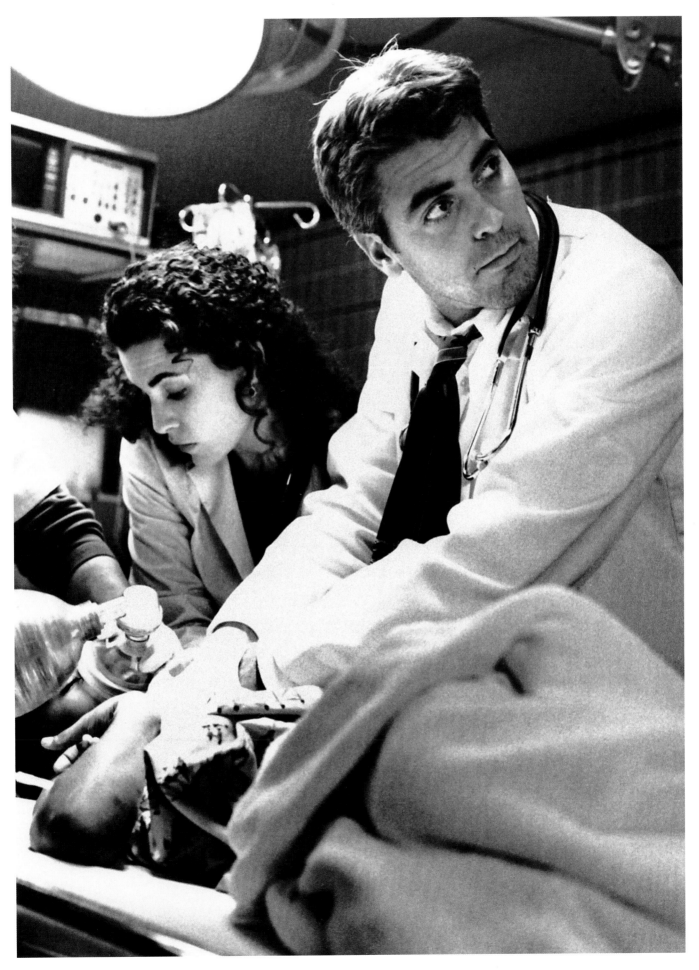

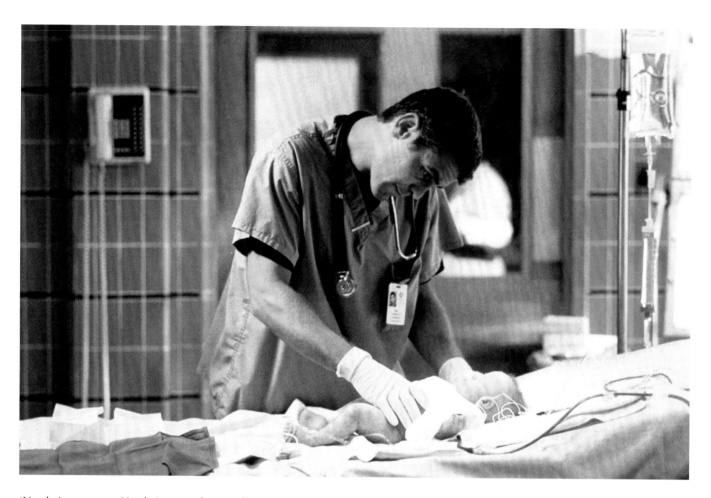

'Yes, he's gorgeous. Yes, he's canny, he's intelligent, he's well dressed. He's also deeply loyal. He has no time for pretension and laziness and arrogance. He has incredible grace.'[15] All of this came rushing off the television screen in the first few seasons of *ER*, and every suspicion of human perfection was confirmed by the admiring magazine profiles that attended this first blush of stardom. If, as Pauline Kael once observed, 'Everyone likes the idea of Cary Grant',[16] the same seems true of Clooney. This being the case, surely they would line up for any movie to which his name was attached. Now that the secret of George Clooney was out, the big-screen payoff was certain to be immediate and immense.

Of 'TV George' and 'Movie George'

'In TV I learned to focus on the script,' recalls Clooney, 'but I didn't apply that lesson to movies. But the cliché is true: You can take a good script and make a bad movie. But you can't take a bad script and make a good movie.'[17] This was certainly true of his 1980s horror work (the unfinished *Grizzly II: The Concert*, *Return to Horror High* and *Return of the Killer Tomatoes!*), but with the exception of 1997's truly lousy *Batman & Robin*, it is a stretch to suggest Clooney fell victim to a series of bad screenplays as he struggled to segue from television star to movie star. While still committed to *ER*, Clooney quickly rattled off

four features: *From Dusk Till Dawn* (1996), *One Fine Day* (1996), *Batman & Robin* and *The Peacemaker* (1997). These films were released within a nineteen-month span, showcasing Clooney as, respectively, a violent criminal, a rakish journalist, Batman and a US Special Forces anti-terror expert – and aside from the caped crusader debacle, they are solid entertainments. *From Dusk Till Dawn*, Quentin Tarantino's screenwriting follow-up to his pop cultural juggernaut *Pulp Fiction* (1994), fared the best with critics, with *Variety*'s Todd McCarthy raving over Clooney's 'instant emergence as a full-fledged movie star'.[18] Seeing Clooney in a motion picture with legitimate pedigree (no matter how low its aim) must have been a shock to the system for McCarthy, as Clooney is doing little more than a vicious, mildly psychotic variation on Dr. Ross.

This is an important distinction to make: 'TV George' is the dashing fellow with the Caesar haircut prowling the emergency room with his head cocked to the side (usually to the left, but the right will do), mellifluously rattling off a mouthful of dialogue with such pleasing elan the viewer does not much care that it is more affectation than acting. This works fine on *ER*, and is acceptable in a decent romantic comedy like *One Fine Day* (Roger Ebert astutely shrugged it off as 'Mel Gibson lite'[19]), where Clooney gets to knock around B-minus banter with a top-notch performer like Michelle Pfeiffer, but it feels like

Above: Clooney fought to get *ER*, the medical drama that makes him a star.

Opposite: George Clooney stars in Robert Rodriguez's *From Dusk Till Dawn* (1996).

a crutch in a red-meat actors' piece like the first half of *From Dusk Till Dawn*. Before the Robert Rodriguez-directed horror flick descends into bloodsucking chaos, Clooney is given ample space to make Seth Gecko more than a tattooed tough guy who routinely backs up his psychopath brother (Quentin Tarantino) despite objecting to his sibling's sadistic behaviour. But when exchanging dim views on the human condition with a widowed ex-minister (Harvey Keitel), whose family the Geckos have taken hostage, Clooney is all TV tics. It is a grandstanding star turn where genuine acting is required; despite his amply demonstrated capacity for violence, Clooney's murderer comes off as a fidgety lightweight compared to the stillness of Keitel's been-there, lost-that father. But he was new to the medium, so critics were willing to overlook Clooney's cruise-control performance. 'Not many television actors make the transition easily,' observed Janet Maslin, 'but not many look this much like Cary Grant.'[20]

Waste Not

Clooney has been remarkably available to journalists over the course of his career, but when these writers have been granted an audience (typically at the Studio City house Clooney purchased back when *ER* first hit; a house that, once he has moved on, will be notable for having been lived in by George Clooney *and* Clark Gable), they seem seduced into accepting the same biographical details Clooney has happily doled out since the public took an interest in his personal life. 'Handling success well is a trick', cautions Clooney. 'I've got a great advantage because my Aunt Rosemary was very successful at a very young age in the '50s, and she didn't handle it well. She paid a very heavy price for it for a long period of time – probably about 20 years, she sort of dropped off the face of the earth. And then she came back roaring and was great. But she had a tough time of it. So I got a really good lesson in the idea that all of this is fleeting. Anyone who thinks that success is a permanent state, particularly in my line of work, is just an idiot. I know what the journey is, and I want to try and enjoy it while I can.'[21] Clooney also throws in the story of his Great Uncle George Guilfoyle, the World War II veteran for whom he was named, and at whose bedside Clooney was present when he died. Guilfoyle's last words, 'What a waste',[22] have echoed throughout Clooney's life, and he has clearly avoided the profound regret expressed by his namesake.

Give Clooney the time and he will gladly discuss his commitment to protecting the innocent civilians of Sudan caught in the bloody crossfire of the region's ongoing civil war. He will take good-natured shots at his movie star pals Brad Pitt, Don Cheadle and Matt Damon, and talk trash about Leonardo DiCaprio's pickup basketball team (which Clooney's team once decimated in a *somewhat* friendly game). He will show reporters around his swanky Studio City home (once the most coveted bachelor pad in Los Angeles), including the back patio where his beloved 300-pound pot-bellied pig, Max, used to roam. He will entertain questions about his dating history (which officially ended with his marriage to Amal Alamuddin in September 2014), and politely decline to kiss and tell. He will do what George Clooney has done his whole life: he will win them over.

What he will not do, or, at least, has not done – perhaps because it seems insignificant when interviewing a gentleman of his global eminence and preternatural charm – is discuss in detail how he suddenly became one of the best actors on the planet. In September 1997, audiences were treated to one last 'TV George' performance in *The Peacemaker*, an action-laden geopolitical thriller so dense with incident that Clooney and co-star Nicole Kidman never have time to do more than react to the surrounding calamities (staged with muscular aplomb by frequent *ER* director Mimi Leder). And yet there is a moment during a ferocious gun battle in a Vienna plaza where Clooney, outnumbered by Russian mobsters, emerges from his totalled automobile and ruthlessly empties the clip of his pistol into the chest of a thug trapped in a burning car. This is a different, decisive George Clooney. There are no tics and no jokes – just a pitiless execution carried out by a violent man. And it was the most exhilarating scene of Clooney's career up until that point because it was completely unexpected. He was not asking the audience to love him in this moment; he was looking to be feared (*sans* the wink-and-nod safety net of *From Dusk Till Dawn*). It was not exactly Paul Newman going full anti-hero as Hud (*Hud*, 1963), but it was a bracing display of ruthlessness that suggested there might be a remorseless killer under the impeccably dressed, finely coiffed exterior.

There is a lot more to George Clooney, the actor, than many realize – mostly because he has given some of his most un-Clooney-like performances in box-office disappointments or flops. Though he is wonderfully vulnerable in films like *Up in the Air* (2009) and *The Descendants* (2011), he is yet to match the emotional rawness of *Solaris* (2002). And while he justly won a Best Supporting Actor Oscar for playing a past-his-prime CIA operative in *Syriana* (2005), he was so much more haunted and diminished as a dead-ended corporate fixer in *Michael Clayton* (2007). Clooney has range, but, having wandered the Hollywood wilderness early in his career, he has also developed a keen sense of his own limitations. He will pile on the pounds and facial hair if he can find his way into the role, but he is never going to be a chameleon. He is the best type

Opposite: George Clooney plays in *The Peacemaker* (1997), a thriller starring also Nicole Kidman, and directed by Mimi Leder.

Following pages: George Clooney in *The Monuments Men* (2014), his fifth film as director.

Opposite: George Clooney in *The Good German* (2006) by Steven Soderbergh.

Above: George Clooney in *Burn After Reading* (2008), a comedy by Joel and Ethan Coen.

of movie star, the kind who is aware of his allure, and, while not apologetic for it, would prefer not to lean on his effortless charm. He enjoys playing the fool (especially for Joel and Ethan Coen) and appears to have a taste for darker material, provided the audience is there for it (which, sadly, it was not for the underrated *The American*, 2010). He is also unusually generous. Not many actors of his stature are so indifferent to franchising out their persona, and it is telling that, when he did bother with a film series, he turned it into an all-star hang-out session with the *Ocean's* movies. This is the Clooney way: he is inclusive, selfless and ambitious. He is, as his parents drilled into him at an early age, an incredibly fortunate man and he has no intention of squandering his time in the sun.

1

Jack Foley

Out of Sight (1998)
Steven Soderbergh

'We didn't have that thing, you know that…
that spark, you know. You gotta have that.'
—Jack Foley

While a stress-ridden Clooney was nursing a
bleeding ulcer brought on by his participation
in the tumultuous first season of *Roseanne* in
1988 (where he played Booker Brooks, the boss
and eventual romantic interest of Laurie Metcalf's
Jackie), a bright young filmmaker was quietly
fomenting the second American independent
film revolution on a no-frills movie set in Baton
Rouge, Louisiana. Budgeted at $1.2 million,
Sex, Lies, and Videotape (1989) would soon
make its twenty-six-year-old writer–director,
Steven Soderbergh, a much-desired wunderkind
in the fickle fields of Hollywood. By the end
of 1989, the upstart auteur had taken home the
Audience Award at the Sundance Film Festival
and won the prestigious Palme d'or from the
Cannes Film Festival (then the youngest to ever
receive the top prize). In March 1990, Soderbergh
would receive an Academy Award nomination
for Best Original Screenplay. It was a precipitous
rise, but, by 1994, when Clooney landed his
breakthrough role on *ER*, Soderbergh had
followed up *Sex, Lies, and Videotape* with
two major flops (*Kafka* [1991] and *King of
the Hill* [1993]), while a third, *The Underneath*
(1995), was on the way. By now, if Soderbergh
was discussed at all in Hollywood, it was usually
as the subject of a 'Whatever happened to…'
query.

As Clooney's star shot heavenward,
Soderbergh's career began to take on the
appearance of a cautionary tale; he was a brilliant
director who had mistaken personal taste for
commercial appeal, subsequently squandering
the excitement generated by his début film.
The movies were not bad or uninteresting (*King
of the Hill* remains one of Soderbergh's finest
pictures), but audiences simply were not in the
mood for a Kafka-esque noir, an unsentimental
Depression-era coming-of-age story or a cold-
around-the-heart heist flick. If, however, that is
the kind of material a filmmaker is drawn to,
it might make sense to sell it to the public via
the high-wattage charm of a bona fide movie star.
The trick for Soderbergh was finding one who
matched his sensibilities.

Butch Cassidy and the Augusta Kid

In the ideal version of George Clooney and
Steven Soderbergh meeting for the first time,
one imagines a scene of two cagey, kindred spirits
sizing each other up for a brief moment before
cheerfully emptying a bottle of top-shelf bourbon
over a lively discussion of 1970s American
cinema, baseball and practical jokes (both
gentlemen are inveterate pranksters). According
to Soderbergh, the encounter was a little more
formal than that: 'I met him in a group. He was
with his agent at the time and [Jersey Films
producers] Danny DeVito, Michael Shamberg
and Stacey Sher. I was sort of auditioning for
the room.'[23] The producers knew they wanted
Clooney for the 'gentleman bank robber' role
of Jack Foley long before they had considered
Soderbergh as a potential director. But while the
basic idea of Clooney as a dashing rogue sounds
like a home run now, Hollywood was in a very
different place with the actor in 1997. 'I know
in some cases there were some people that they
had approached about doing *Out of Sight* who
declined because they were not convinced George
was a movie star', remembers Soderbergh.[24]

Based on the novel of the same name by Elmore
Leonard, *Out of Sight* was, on the page, a spiky,
sexy crime yarn that pitted the likeable scoundrel
Foley (George Clooney) against no-nonsense
United States Marshal Karen Sisco (Jennifer
Lopez). Written by Scott Frank, it was an aesthetic
continuation of sorts to *Get Shorty* (1995, also
adapted by Frank), which had transformed the
tomes of Elmore Leonard into hot Hollywood
properties overnight; finally, after decades of
swift book sales, the film industry had cracked
the Leonard code, and everyone wanted a piece
of the verbose tough-guy action. Eager to replicate
their success with Leonard, Danny DeVito's
Jersey Films acquired the rights to *Out of Sight*,
and brought the project to Universal Pictures,
where, after *Get Shorty* director Barry Sonnenfeld
passed, executive Casey Silver fought to attach
Soderbergh. Though Jersey Films required some
convincing that Soderbergh, given his brutal
box-office history, was the right man for the job,
they were not about to hold Clooney's string
of big-screen disappointments against him.
After all, 'gentleman bank robber' sounded like

In Steven Soderbergh's
Out of Sight (1998), Clooney
plays Jack Foley, a charming
ex-con.

an alternative-universe line of work for Clooney (and only the most hardened Leonard-phile would complain that, following the book, Foley should be a well-seasoned fifty). So why were other directors reticent to accept Clooney as a viable leading man? 'I think there are a couple of factors that are impossible to tell by just looking at someone in a TV show or a movie', says Soderbergh. 'You may think, "Oh, they have certain qualities that lend themselves to being a movie star", but what you don't know is what they're like as people. In the case of George, his taste, his ambition and his fearlessness were something that I only came to know through working with him. That's not stuff you can tell just by looking at somebody, and those are three crucial components in his success.'[25] Another factor that might have scared off other filmmakers: Clooney's seeming inability to modulate his TV tics; he had yet to prove he could stifle them for an entire film, and most filmmakers, particularly those chasing studio gigs, would prefer to do as little 'directing' of an actor as possible.

So Clooney needed Soderbergh as much as the director needed the job. 'We found each other at the right time', said Soderbergh. 'I think in that moment, we were both perceived as not living up to our potential, and we both felt we had a lot on the line.'[26] Soderbergh's travails were certainly more dire: he had been consigned to the art-house ghetto (a fate he seemed to embrace with the experimental satire of 1996's *Schizopolis*), and had to prove he could craft an accessible, if not bankable movie. 'I reached a point where, pre-*Out of Sight*, I realized, "Wow, half the business is off limits to me. I don't like that. That seems dumb. That seems like not a good career trajectory." So when *Out of Sight* showed up, I thought, "Okay, I know how to do this, and I *need* to do this. I want to do it. I can do it."'[27]

As a savvy student of film, Soderbergh had zero doubts about Clooney's leading-man qualities: he immediately saw the star-making potential of Clooney as Jack Foley, likening the timing of the role to Robert Redford's 1969 breakthrough in *Butch Cassidy and the Sundance Kid*. 'Redford before *Butch Cassidy* was an actor people thought well of and thought should be a movie star and yet he wasn't somehow. It took seeing him in a role that showed you what he could do. It's material – it's all about material. If there are talented actors out there who haven't made it yet, it's just that they're not getting access to good material. George hasn't been big just because of the parts. [*Batman & Robin* and *The Peacemaker*] are not showcases for an actor. I felt he really needed one. [...] Jack Foley for any actor is a great role, but this is his Butch Cassidy.'[28] Only, Butch Cassidy never possessed the stupid courage to hold up a bank without a gun.

Unarmed Robbery

Published in 1996, Leonard's *Out of Sight* opens with Jack Foley tunnelling out of a medium-security prison in Florida, where he expects his partner-in-crime, Buddy Bragg (Ving Rhames), will be waiting for him. Though Buddy is indeed on the other side of the tunnel, there is also a shotgun-wielding federal marshal named Karen Sisco hanging out in the parking lot tending to unrelated business. Jack and Buddy get the drop on Karen and stow her in the trunk – where Jack was to hide by himself until Buddy had made it a safe distance from the penitentiary. Now, the rakish burglar has cramped company, and he cannot help but ply his charm on this uncommonly gorgeous law enforcement official; it is both a meet-close and a meet-cute. But what plays smashingly in the book might have felt like too much, too soon in the movie – which runs a hair over two hours and is driven largely by the idiosyncratic behaviour of its characters. So Soderbergh cleverly delays the trunk-bound seduction until later in the film's first act, which gives him time to establish Jack's gift for smooth talk and Karen's romantic frustrations (namely her affair with a not-quite-divorced fellow agent).

Soderbergh's restructuring of the plot quickly reveals what every other director had done wrong with Clooney up until that point. All one needs to do is place him in a compelling scenario with some crisp dialogue and the audience will follow him anywhere. In *Out of Sight*, Soderbergh opens with an amusingly flustered Jack stomping out of an office building and flinging his tie to the ground – an image deemed suitable for freeze-framing over the title card. This is a frazzled, thwarted Clooney; there is no self-satisfied cocking of the head, nor does he resort to that mischievous grin (at least, not yet). Instead, Clooney's Jack Foley adjusts his jacket, affects a toothy sneer and lumbers like an oaf across the street to the SunTrust Bank, which, in a fit of self-destructive pique, he intends to rob without a gun. What occurs inside the bank is easy enough for Clooney: he sweet-talks an adorable young teller into believing that a man he does not know is, in fact, his partner, who has orders to shoot her assistant manager if she fails to do precisely as he says. She buys his story straightaway and Jack further earns the viewer's affections by quickly putting her at ease, assuring her she is 'doing great' as he gently asks her not to remove any bills from the bottom of the drawer. Once she complies, Jack is on his way with an envelope full of money; Clooney reprises his awkward Frankenstein gait as he exits the bank (Soderbergh calls it 'George's funny walk' on the movie's DVD commentary), and hops in a car that, of course, will not start. Two things are true by the end of this scene: Jack is going back to jail, and George Clooney will never be mistaken for anything other than a movie star.

Hey Yourself

Universal Studios might have been sold on
Clooney as Jack Foley from the very beginning,
but they were far from certain about who should
play Karen Sisco. Had the studio won the casting
battle, Clooney would have had an on-screen
dalliance with a future co-star. 'Sandra [Bullock]
was one of the people we were all talking about',
said Soderbergh. 'What happened was I spent
some time with [Clooney and Bullock] – and they
actually did have a great chemistry. But it was for
the wrong movie. They really should do a movie
together, but it was not Elmore Leonard energy.'[29]

Soderbergh and Clooney met with many
actresses throughout the casting process, but only
one could go quip-for-quip with Jack Foley in
a manner that was as sexy as it was intimidating.
Though Jennifer Lopez had received mostly
positive reviews for her portrayal of slain Tejano
recording artist Selena in the self-titled biopic,
Universal wanted a more established performer
for Karen; this prompted Soderbergh and Clooney
to dig in their heels and insist on Lopez. 'What
convinced me was that George was better with
Jennifer than with anybody else. George and
Jennifer in a room, *that's* the energy this movie
needs.'[30] In a couple of years, Lopez would be
a platinum recording artist and this would have
been a no-brainer, but in 1997 it was a battle; had
Universal prevailed, it is possible two of Clooney's

best scenes would have fallen flat, undercutting
the effectiveness of that opening robbery and
knocking his bid for big-screen stardom back to
square one. 'I think George and I bonded pretty
quickly over the casting of the female lead', says
Soderbergh, 'Because we saw almost everybody
in town, and we were both convinced that Jennifer
was the right person for the part, and we had to
fight for that.'[31]

When Gary Met Celeste

When Soderbergh first filmed the trunk flirtation
between Jack and Karen, he insisted on staging it
all in one uninterrupted take, believing that the
camera-fogging heat of his actors would be so
overpowering that audiences would not notice
the duration of the shot; this was, in essence, the
noodling show-off of *Kafka* attempting to stunt
the maturity of a great director badly in need of a
commercial success. Nevertheless, Soderbergh got
his way, burning through forty-four takes before
he finally nailed the scene; after a disastrous test
screening where recruited viewers registered
confusion and outright contempt for the long-
playing sequence, Soderbergh went back and
re-shot the version of the scene that has become
one of cinema's greatest on-screen flirtations.

The technical craft of the scene is worthy of
a chapter in and of itself, but its most remarkable
element is Clooney's refusal to play it cool.

Above: US Marshal Karen
Sisco (Jennifer Lopez) snugly
held hostage by Jack Foley in
the trunk of a car.

Opposite: Joel Schumacher's
Batman & Robin, a film that
Clooney would regret for the
rest of his life.

Following pages: Watch your
back, Jack.

There is no case to be made for Joel Schumacher's franchise-hobbling *Batman & Robin* (1997): it is a tacky parade of camped-up superhero movie tropes that should have starred a Vegas magician and his plucky assistant, not George Clooney and Chris O'Donnell. It is the kind of breathtakingly lavish Hollywood spectacle that is so contemptuously enervating as to make one angry at the pricey misappropriation of creative energy. Only Uma Thurman, as the deadly horticulturist Poison Ivy, emerges with a shred of dignity left clinging to her hideously designed outfit.

Knowing he would never live down the infamy of *Batman & Robin*, Clooney quickly disowned the film; to this day, he will gladly dish out a single-serving of invective to remind fans and critics that no one is more aware of the movie's awfulness than he is: 'I call it the Jack Kennedy syndrome. The first thing he did was the Bay of Pigs. A complete failure. But he never tried to hide from it. He admitted his mistake, and he moved on. *Batman & Robin* was terrible, and I was terrible in it.'[a] Granted, it is hard to call a statement in which somebody compares himself to John F. Kennedy an egoless concession of failure, but there is also this: 'I watch *Batman & Robin* from time to time. It's the worst movie I ever made so it's a good lesson in humility.'[b] Like Muhammad Ali obsessively studying tape of his ignominious defeat to Joe Frazier in 1971, this is Clooney reminding himself that even self-aware hubris (in the service of a very good pay cheque) will not go unpunished. A movie star's presence in a film should serve as a guarantee of quality; in the case of *Batman & Robin*, it was a signifier of sloth.

There is no reason to criticize Clooney for appearing uninterested or lost in *Batman & Robin* because the entire enterprise is a lost cause. *The Wall Street Journal*'s Joe Morgenstern offered faint praise, claiming, 'Of all modern Batmans, George Clooney bears the closest physical resemblance to the comic-book hero, but there isn't much to say about his performance because there isn't much performance to discuss.'[c] Clooney is blunt when discussing his involvement in the film that forced Warner Bros. to completely reboot the series: 'They say I was a bad Batman, that it was my fault. They say I buried the franchise. But the truth is, it was a $150 million film and they paid me $10 million.'[d] It is around this time that something clicked for Clooney. He looked around, saw that he had a top-rated cushion called *ER* running on television and realized the film business was more passion than obligation. In 2014 he summarized the epiphany thus: 'How much money do you need? I own my house. I don't live above my means. So it's more fun to do the projects you want to do and have something you're proud of when all is said and done.'[e]

Opposite: All Jack and Karen
want is each other, as is evoked
in this steamy, dreamy bathtub
seduction and later in a scene
(bottom) when Jack and
Buddy elude the Feds at
the hotel.

Following pages: A romantic
rendezvous in Detroit.

As he jostles around in the trunk, situated behind a plainly revolted Karen, Jack comes off as an uncouth doofus who thinks he is a lot smarter than he really is. Perhaps it is the high of the successful prison escape, but Jack exudes an unearned surfeit of confidence as he rifles through Karen's belongings; Karen, on the other hand, is disgusted with herself, furious that she let a clod like Jack get the better of her. But Jack's gregariousness gradually turns endearing, largely because Clooney loves playing the fool; in a way, he is giving audiences a glimpse of the dim-witted vanity that repeatedly gets *O Brother, Where Art Thou?*'s Ulysses Everett McGill and his cohorts into more figurative 'tight spots'. But the longer Jack rambles on, loudly misquoting Peter Finch's iconic outburst from *Network* (1976), the more he disarms Karen; he is a career criminal, but he is utterly harmless. And yet Karen has to redeem her professional pride, so the minute he slips up exiting the trunk, she draws down on him. This only heightens Jack's excitement, and Clooney plays it beautifully as a man too turned on to worry about self-preservation.

As *Out of Sight* glides into its second act, it becomes apparent that Clooney has effectively killed off 'TV George'. The head never bobbles, the line readings are consistently natural and he simply looks more relaxed than ever. How did Soderbergh break Clooney of his oft-lamented small-screen habits? 'It wasn't a big thing', he says. 'The first thing we shot as I recall was this prison library scene with George and Don Cheadle and Albert Brooks, where Don is shaking Albert down for money. I just said, "Be still. You've got great stuff to say, you've got great actors around. Just be still. Take your time." That was it. That was all I ever said about that. He went, "I got it." It was never anything more than that. I didn't have a big plan. I assumed going in that he would be open to doing what the scene required as opposed to "This is what I always do." He struck me as somebody who wanted to be directed, and it's my job to have the universe of the movie figured out. That was really it. It was a ten-second conversation.'[32] This approach is the exact opposite of the one David O. Russell would undertake with Clooney the following year on *Three Kings*, but more on that in the subsequent chapter.

Out of Sight's centrepiece is the skilfully edited, deliciously sensual sequence in which Jack tracks down Karen at a luxury hotel in Detroit, Michigan. She is there in pursuit of him, while he is in town preparing to pull off a theft that could very well end in the longest prison sentence of his life, and all they want is each other. It is essentially an erotic rendition of the De Niro/Pacino tête-à-tête in *Heat* (1995); hunter and hunted calling a 'time out' to scratch a wicked itch that has been driving them crazy since they wound up spooning in the trunk of a car together. Soderbergh has built to this moment masterfully, dropping in an earlier dream sequence where Karen catches Jack luxuriating in a steaming hot bath; intrigued, she lets her guard down and makes out with the thief before being roused in her hospital bed by her baffled father (Dennis Farina). Ever since the escape, they have been obsessed with an impossible coupling and now, as snowflakes drift by their delicately lit reflections in a high-rise window, they have an opportunity. 'It's like seeing someone for the first time', says Jack. 'You could be passing on the street. You look at each other for a few seconds, and there's this kind of recognition like you both know something. Next moment the person's gone, and it's too late to do anything about it.' Karen takes a deep sip of her whiskey neat, while David Holmes's score provides a languorous prelude to lovemaking. This is when Soderbergh begins to skip back and forth, like a master DJ, from hotel-bar seduction to hotel-room fulfilment. 'It would be worth the risk', says Jack. Clooney is delivering his dialogue at something just above a whisper, as if he is a nose-length away on the adjacent pillow; it is Cary Grant pitching close-quarters woo to Ingrid Bergman in *Notorious* (1946). This is the stuff. This is the smouldering seduction viewers had been waiting for since Clooney first appeared on their television sets – only, Clooney gives the foreplay a characteristically dorky tweak when he apologetically drops his trousers to reveal a blindingly white pair of boxer shorts. Lopez's non-verbal reaction is perfect, veering from are-you-kidding-me disbelief to I'll-allow-it amusement; it is the sexiest fashion *faux pas* ever. Then they are in each other's arms and it is everything movies do better than real life.

Miles to Go

Despite an abundance of enthusiastically positive reviews, *Out of Sight* failed to connect with audiences in its initial release. Universal strangely sold the film with a hand-painted poster that was unusually stylish for the era, depicting a leggy Jennifer Lopez brandishing a shotgun against a yellow and red background primarily occupied by a rugged looking George Clooney. It was a bold, classy choice for a film that needed to separate itself from the CG-laden competition of summer 1998, but moviegoers flocked to *The X-Files* and *Armageddon* instead. And yet there was an understanding in Hollywood that *Out of Sight* was a film of such tremendous quality that, had it been released in the fall, it probably would have been a sizeable hit. Soderbergh had resurrected his career, while Clooney had at last delivered the full-fledged movie-star performance audiences had been expecting for close to a decade. Roger Ebert summed it up best in his three-and-a-half-star (out of four) review: 'A lot of actors who are handsome when young need to put on some miles

Above and opposite: Jack
faces a long ride back to
Florida, but he will 'have
a lot to talk about' with his
travelling companion.

before the full flavor emerges; observe how Nick
Nolte, Mickey Rourke, Harrison Ford and Clint
Eastwood moved from stereotypes to individuals.
Here Clooney at last looks like a big screen star;
the good-looking leading man from television is
over with.'[33]

Most importantly, Clooney had forged a strong
creative bond with Soderbergh, who placed
an equally high premium on quality projects.
'I started out [in Maysville Pictures] with a nice
guy who had the old producer ideal – you get
thirty-five projects in development and do two
or three of them', said Clooney. 'I looked at all
the projects and said, "I wouldn't do any of these."
When that deal was up, I said to Steven, "Look,
let's do movies we want to do." It was a way for
me to protect Steven and for Steven to protect me.
He's got great taste.'[34]

It would be three years before Clooney and
Soderbergh would join forces again, but both
were reinvigorated creatively; when they did
reunite for *Ocean's Eleven* in 2001, Soderbergh
had won an Academy Award for *Traffic* (2000),
while Clooney had enjoyed his first runaway
commercial success with *The Perfect Storm*
(2000). But the greatest challenge to Clooney's
public persona and, in some ways, acting ability
was waiting for him in the desert southwest of
the United States (Arizona), where a brilliant,
yet volatile filmmaker was gearing up to make
his own major artistic leap.

2

Archie Gates

Three Kings (1999)
David O. Russell

'The way it works is, you do the thing you're scared shitless of, and you get the courage *after* you do it, not before you do it.'
—Archie Gates

One of the major recurring themes of Clooney's early stardom is combat: he 'fought' to get on *ER*, and he 'fought' for the right to play Jack Foley in *Out of Sight*, and he would continue to fight for roles in artistically ambitious films made by talented directors. This brawling mentality is a by-product of his Kentucky upbringing; he was taught to stand up for himself and others (especially the marginalized) and to push back if pushed. So when Clooney heard about a Gulf War heist flick called *Three Kings* gearing up at Warner Bros. with the up-and-coming filmmaker David O. Russell at the helm, he strapped on the boxing gloves and aggressively let it be known that his services were available for the co-lead role of Sergeant Major Archie Gates. Standing in his way was one considerable impediment: Russell viewed Clooney as a tic-reliant TV actor and, therefore, wanted no part of the actor in his film.

For a film set amid the chaos of an absurd war, the process of making *Three Kings* – from script to postproduction – was suitably insane. It was a battleground of ego, reckless invention and good old Hollywood politics – a defiantly unconventional wrench in the studio gears that was nearly thwarted by risk-averse company men every step of the way. It was, put simply, an accident: Bill Gerber, the executive who had encouraged Russell to indulge his anarchic muse while rewriting John Ridley's original screenplay (initially titled *Spoils of War*), was fired before casting began, leaving the typically conservative Lorenzo di Bonaventura as the director's sole protector against a studio desperate to squash the project. It was Russell's big opportunity to make the leap from the indie film world to the Hollywood A-list, but his fiery temperament placed him at odds not only with executives but his cast and crew as well. He felt as though compromise was being forced upon him throughout, and thus was hostile to nearly every suggestion that ran counter to his creative vision. One such compromise was Clooney: Russell wanted Nicolas Cage for Archie Gates, but was open to the idea of Clint Eastwood,

John Travolta, Mel Gibson and, as a last ditch effort to keep Clooney off the film, Dustin Hoffman. But the studio was pushing Clooney, and Russell was pushing back.

Clooney was pushing, too, and he had leverage; he had recently signed a long-term production deal with Warner Bros. and the studio had every intention of keeping him happy. Russell, however, was stuck on 'TV George', an idea that was only exacerbated by his mother-in-law, who once asked him 'Clooney? Isn't he that guy who's always squinting on that TV show?'[35] But Clooney loved Russell's subversive take on the tale of four US soldiers who go AWOL hunting for Saddam Hussein's gold bullion in the immediate aftermath of the Gulf War's resolution. The project fit Clooney's post-*Batman & Robin* criterion of quality-over-massive-payday. 'If the movie makes money, you make money', he told *Playboy* in 2000. 'If it doesn't, you make the movie anyway.'[36] And Clooney was willing to roll the dice on a pay cut, with a piece of the potential backend, to play the fun-loving, screw-happy Special Forces officer whose venal subordination results in a moral awakening. So every time Russell vacillated on casting him, Clooney pushed back. Hard.

Memo to David O. Russell

One of the most charming aspects of Clooney's personality is his Old Hollywood affection for letter writing. He is an avid scribbler of missives, most of which are playful and, at times, mischievously fired off on letterhead bearing another person's name (most notably Brad Pitt's). At the moment of Russell's casting of *Three Kings*, this habit served two purposes: it established his self-deprecating sense of humour, while reassuring the director that he was actively committed to making a great film. Here is Clooney's handwritten pitch to Russell in full:

'I was on the set of *Batman & Robin* when I saw a tape of *Flirting with Disaster*. I remember thinking how similar the two films were. When I heard you were developing a film at Warner Bros., I called Lorenzo and said I wanted in. I hadn't read the script. Now I have. So I know basically what's going on. Tom Cruise! Makes sense to me. And if his dance card is full I don't know who you have next on your list. I know I'm not on it.

George Clooney as Archie
Gates in *Three Kings*,
David O. Russell's 1999 film.

35

Opposite: Gates studies the 'Iraqi Ass Map'.

Above: Clooney had to fight to win over director David O. Russell.

Following pages: They have come to steal the stolen gold. Gates stands, Private First Class Conrad Vig (Spike Jonze) has the wheel and Sergeant First Class Troy Barlow (Mark Wahlberg) is in flight.

(And with films like *Batman* I don't blame you.) But I couldn't sleep at night if I let a project this good go away without making one attempt. I just finished a film with Steven Soderbergh and Scott Frank. It kicks ass. That doesn't necessarily mean that I kick ass. But I think I did alright. What I know is, that I could screen it for you. Even toss in some Goobers. You'll get who you want for this. I just didn't want an agent or a studio trying to sell you on me. I can screw this up all by myself. —George Clooney, TV Actor[37]'

It was a pleasantly witty gesture, but the fact of the matter is that Russell was bereft of other options: the studio wanted their star in the picture and that eventually became non-negotiable. But when Russell finally gave in, he managed to place some heavy preconditions on his star. 'You have a lot of habits, you ought to break them', Russell told Clooney. 'Let's work together before we go into production, because I don't think you're going to want to have me changing these habits in front of a hundred people.'[38] Clooney acquiesced, which led to him engaging in meditation and breathing exercises during his downtime on *ER*. It was Russell's hope that this process would ease the actor out of his Dr. Ross persona, which the filmmaker diagnoses as follows on the *Three Kings* DVD commentary track: 'George had developed a style of acting on *ER* in which his first instinct in most scenes was to not look at the person he was talking to. This technique

of George's was fine. It worked great on *ER*. But that was the habit that we were both working to change in this movie. It's hard when it's a well-established habit, because he learned to be most comfortable remembering dialogue that way, and getting into the feeling of the dialogue that way.'[39]

Clooney was game for anything Russell requested at first, but soon grew weary of the director's demands, which included memorizing ever-changing dialogue. Russell was riding Clooney extremely hard, which is peculiar if indeed he took the time to screen *Out of Sight*. If he had watched the film, he would have seen that Clooney had completely shed his TV tics under Soderbergh's direction. (Soderbergh is not aware as to whether Russell saw his film beforehand, but he did talk to the director: 'I remember having a conversation with David in which I raved about George.'[40]) Clooney likely knew this, but his inclination for diplomacy compelled him to address the matter with Russell in a generally good-natured letter:

'David, Just wanted to send you a quick note. First to say how excited I am about this project. I know it's years of work for you. It shows. I also want you to know I'll do the best I can to work with your process. It's not how I work. That doesn't mean it's wrong, it's just new to me. So I'll give you all I got. You won't win on all of them, because I'm also doing the show. And you're going to have to understand. If there's something I can't

do, you can bet it's because I'm working [on *ER*]. Now there's something you can do for me. Get me the script. I need time to work on it. To break it down. It's the most important thing you can do to help my performance. The sooner I get it the better I'll be. I know you're getting worked from every angle but see what you can do. Thanks, George (honorable TV's Dr. Ross)[41]'

This was the state of Clooney's relationship with Russell as the project commenced principal photography in the fall of 1998, and it deteriorated rapidly under the blazing heat of a sixty-eight-day shoot in the Arizona desert. What occurred on the set is a matter of differing interpretations, but this much is certain: after weeks of tension and bickering, there was a physical altercation between Clooney and Russell over the alleged mistreatment of extras. The two were separated and forced to shake hands, but this was just the beginning of a decade-long feud; in the meantime, Warner Bros. sent a physical production executive[42] to ensure that the shoot did not veer too far off-schedule (they wound up wrapping a forgivable five days late). There is probably a book or a *Hearts of Darkness*-style documentary[43] to be made out of the tumultuous production of *Three Kings*. It is not, however, the purpose of this book, so, in the interest of fairness and clarity, let us place the focus on the film itself, which, despite the turmoil, now stands as one of the finest American war films ever made.

Iraqi Ass Map

If the notion that Operation Desert Storm was a righteous response to Iraq's 'naked aggression' seemed fairly specious in 1990, it now plays as a crushingly tragic joke in the wake of the United State's unprovoked invasion of the country in 2003. It is this in-between quality that lends *Three Kings* much of its power: it is both an indictment of failed policies and a prescient satire of much more catastrophic failures to come. And Clooney's Archie Gates is the perfect cynical prism through which to view the hypocrisy and casual inhumanity of this sorry predicament. In the opening moments of the film, the reservists (who will soon be under his charge) chug beer and celebrate the Iraqi forces' withdrawal, while Gates has sex with an opportunistic TV news reporter (Judy Greer) in a makeshift edit bay. He is actually assigned to a different journalist, Adriana Cruz (Nora Dunn), but the bored and horny Gates is not attracted to her, so he is giving what valuable information he has to one of her competitors. When confronted by Cruz, he is unapologetic; the post-war clean-up is of little interest to him and he has little sympathy for a story-crazed journalist desperate to find an angle amid the clamour. Instant gratification trumps anyone else's needs.

On the page, Gates is essentially a feckless Dr. Ross: he is a camo-clad Lothario who is great at his job; the difference with Gates is that he cannot be bothered to do it. There is also a dash of Elliott Gould's cheerfully insubordinate 'Trapper' John McIntyre from *M*A*S*H* in Gates (*Three Kings* frequently recalls the gallows humour of Robert Altman's masterpiece), except the former was a surrogate for the 1960s counterculture. Gates is a post-Reagan anarchist; he is looking to cash in as much as he is to getting laid, but the desert is parched for possibility. There are people getting rich from this war but the soldiers clearly are not in on the windfall – and this is something the close-to-retirement Gates would like to change.

He gets his opportunity when Sergeant First Class Troy Barlow (Mark Wahlberg) discovers a rolled-up piece of paper stuck in the *derrière* of a surrendered Iraqi soldier. Barlow keeps the paper, which appears to be some kind of map, and asks Staff Sergeant Chief Elgin (Ice Cube) for assistance in translating it. Archie happens upon the three soldiers in the midst of their deliberations and declares in no uncertain terms that the map depicts a series of bunkers in which are stashed away loads of gold bullion. This scene is crucial in terms of setting up the parameters of the heist, but it also reveals a new dimension to Clooney's acting. He is still. This may not sound like much, but it is probably one of the hardest things for an actor to do: he conveys authority using nothing but his voice and a fixed gaze. While it is true that the TV tics were abandoned for Jack Foley, he was still able to smile and joke and play a bit of a doofus in Soderbergh's film – all things Clooney loves to do. In this scene he is locked in, which allows him to get the biggest laugh by calmly refuting Private First Class Conrad Vig's (Spike Jonze) ignorant observation that gold bullion is akin to 'them little cubes you put in hot water to make soup'. This is what Russell was trying to pull out of Clooney via yoga exercises on the Warner Bros. lot, and while the intensity of the director's effort may be questionable, the result is not. 'If you watch George's performance,' says the director, 'I think he pulls off this directness beautifully throughout the movie.'[44]

Changing Necessity

Clooney's stillness is the ballast that keeps *Three Kings* steady as it abruptly shifts from caper comedy to conscience-stricken political satire. This occurs when an Iraqi soldier executes a female anti-Saddam dissident in front of her husband, daughter and fellow travellers. Though Gates and the reservists have just retrieved the gold and are ready to split, this act of truly 'naked aggression' cannot go unpunished. A firefight ensues (cleanly shot in individual segments by Russell), leaving numerous Iraqi soldiers dead, while Gates and company are now committed to the well-being of the dissidents. If they leave

Top: Gates with Adriana Cruz (Nora Dunn), a frustrated TV News reporter.

Bottom: Sergeant Major Gates with Barlow, Staff Sergeant Chief Elgin (Ice Cube) and Private Vig.

Following pages: Gates in a fire-fight.

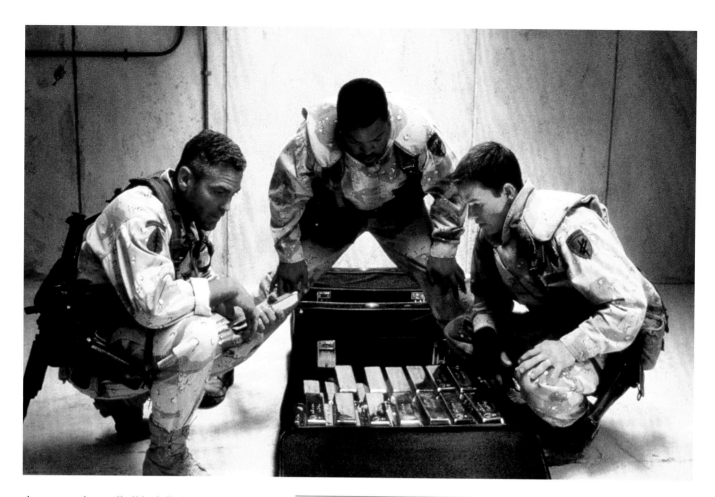

them now, they will all be killed. So they resolve to get these people to safety while still trying to abscond with a life-changing haul of bullion.

Character-wise, the primary arc of *Three Kings* belongs to Wahlberg's Troy Barlow, who is captured and tortured by a vengeful Republican Guard officer whose child was killed in her crib during a US-led air raid. He is at once atoning for having shot a surrendering Iraqi soldier in the first scene in the film (out of confusion, not cruelty) and gaining empathy for a people most Americans know only as enemy combatants. This digression could have easily thrown off the film's strangely propulsive rhythm, but Russell gets away with indulging it because Clooney is still occupying the calm centre of the film; he is driving the main narrative forward (which, amazingly, is no longer about the gold in any compelling way) and maintaining the audience's rooting interest. Gates does not really have much of an arc: the minute he decides to engage the Republican Guard in response to the dissident's execution, he has found purpose in a conflict that had completely disillusioned him. But Clooney, who never stopped believing in the project even when he literally came to blows with its director, is fully invested in the story. This is about serving a unique and important narrative. It is the first time Clooney's political convictions were successfully wedded to quality material.

Shellshock

Though *Three Kings* received almost uniformly glowing reviews from critics, it was completely ignored during the awards season due to Warner Bros.' unwillingness to campaign for it. Clooney vigorously promoted the film, and his performance once again inspired comparisons with Cary Grant – with critic Michael Sragow adroitly noting that 'Archie' was Grant's given name. When asked about the connection, Russell claimed it was a coincidence; in his mind, Clooney's turn reminded him of Grant's more rugged counterpart: 'It's a little bit of a Gary Cooper performance where he doesn't talk a whole lot – but you kind of get his integrity, and his fear and ambivalence at times.'[45] Though Clooney was fed up with Russell behind the scenes, he returned the compliment throughout the press tour by repeatedly praising his director's vision: 'In many ways, the star of the movie is David and David's script.'[46] But Clooney could bite his tongue for only so long. While promoting *The Perfect Storm* the following summer, he spoke candidly about his disdain for Russell's on-set behaviour, calling the shoot 'without exception, the worst experience of my life'.[47] He was still grousing about Russell when speaking with *Vanity Fair* in 2003, which prompted the magazine to seek a response from the director. He obliged with a withering reply: 'George Clooney can suck my dick.'[48]

Above: Gates, Barlow and Elgin have just retrieved Saddam Hussein's gold bullion.

Opposite: Clooney is surrounded by a most formidable cast in *Fail Safe* (2000).

Although Clooney had grown up in and around (and occasionally on) live television, it is *still* a surprise that he would want to risk his unflappable image by attempting the kind of high-wire act that is an adrenaline rush for the performers and a perverse 'Will they blow it?' spectacle for the viewer. While there may be an immediacy and a novelty to the idea of watching famous actors perform live via satellite, it does not quite carry the same tangible charge that makes live theatre such an amazing experience. But Clooney used his expanding clout in 1997 to persuade NBC to open the fourth season of *ER* with a live episode. Largely disconnected from the dangling story threads from the previous season, the episode played as a one-off that concluded with the satisfying sight of its cast and crew celebrating what appeared to be a mistake-free run (though they had to do it all over again for West Coast viewers). The experiment went off without a hitch, but Clooney was not happy with the experience: 'It was my idea to film that episode live, and it didn't really work because we tried to replicate the normal look of the show which you can't do and because we filmed in color which looks like crap because you have to use videotape.'[f] Three years later, Clooney rounded up a murderer's row of actors (including Richard Dreyfuss, Don Cheadle, Harvey Keitel and Brian Dennehy) and had a go at *Fail Safe*, an anti-war drama originally filmed by Sidney Lumet in 1964. Clooney brought back the original screenwriter, Walter Bernstein (a blacklisted scribe who wrote for US TV series *You Are There* in the early '50s), and pulled off a satisfying live broadcast under the direction of Stephen Frears. Though the material, about an accidental nuclear assault on Moscow, was dated, the script and performances were first-rate. It was a throwback triumph for a throwback movie star (who, it is worth noting, has not returned to live-televised drama since).

45

Opposite and above:
Gates rescues a tortured
but still kicking Barlow.

Following pages: Elgin, Barlow
and Gates deliver the Iraqi
refugees safely to the Iranian
border.

For years, the two men took shots at each other in interviews, which was a shame given that their passionate belief in the material was essentially what drove them to clash. 'It's unfortunate for both of them how that thing came out,' said Wahlberg, 'because they were both just trying their best to make the best version of the movie possible.'[49] But Clooney's sense of justice, the same one that forced him to bite that dog when he was a little boy, had been piqued, and for a long time he had zero interest in a reconciliation. Meanwhile, Russell's career took a real hit; he struggled to get productions off the ground until he hit awards-season paydirt with 2010's *The Fighter*. Now that he had earned his way back into Clooney's rarefied territory, the actor at last extended an olive branch. 'I saw David a few weeks ago at a party', Clooney told *The Hollywood Reporter* in 2012. 'There was a bunch of filmmakers there. And I felt compelled to go over and go, "So are we done?" And he goes, "Please." And I said, "OK." Because we made a really, really great film, and we had a really rough time together, but it's a case of both of us getting older. I really do appreciate the work he continues to do, and I think he appreciates what I'm trying to do.'[50] It is a happy ending to a sad story, but it is worth noting that, despite this *détente*, the two have expressed no explicit desire to work together again in the future.

3

Ulysses Everett McGill

O Brother, Where Art Thou? (2000)
Joel Coen

'I'm a Dapper Dan man!'
—Everett

While George Clooney was stuck in Phoenix, Arizona, slogging his way through the filming of *Three Kings*, he received a visit from filmmakers Joel and Ethan Coen, who hand-delivered the screenplay for their next project. Clooney did not need to read the script to know that he wanted to work with the Coens, so he accepted on the spot, without so much as glancing at the cover. It was not until he returned to his hotel that he realized the Coens had chosen him to play Ulysses in their take on Homer's *Odyssey*. 'I couldn't believe my luck', said Clooney.[51]

But if Clooney had dreams of brandishing a sword and felling a man-eating Cyclops, he was about to learn that the Coens were not exactly interested in a classical retelling of Homer's epic poem. Starting with the title, *O Brother, Where Art Thou?*, Clooney must have been both befuddled and elated. It is a specific reference to the fictional film in Preston Sturges's *Sullivan's Travels*, which, though it has little to do with the *Odyssey*, is one of Clooney's all-time favourite movies. As Clooney read the Coens' screenplay, he would certainly find echoes of the 1941 screwball comedy classic; the dialogue occasionally evinces the rapid-fire wit for which Sturges was celebrated, while the three main characters are, like hubristic director John Lloyd Sullivan at the conclusion of his journey, consigned to a chain gang. But the Coens' Depression-era yarn is not wedded to one sensibility; it is a musical adventure through a mythical Mississippi that sings with allusions to works both literary and cinematic. It is, for the Coens, a strangely sincere tribute to the perseverance of the human spirit in the face of poverty, oppression and, depending on one's religious perspective, wrathful Acts of God. And it allowed Clooney the opportunity to slip into the mud-caked skin of a hyper-articulate fool named Ulysses Everett McGill.

We're in a Tight Spot

Clooney's five-year contract on *ER* expired at the end of the show's 1998–9 season and he was adamant that there would be no extension. The show had made him a star and now it was time to fully commit to the career and the medium for which he was, seemingly, genetically born. And yet 1999 was not exactly the most propitious year to cut out the television safety net; aside from the much-maligned *Batman & Robin*, Clooney had yet to achieve true box-office success as a leading man. Bereft of a fallback option, Clooney's movie-star cachet would be tested in the summer of 2000 with Wolfgang Petersen's adaptation of Sebastian Junger's bestseller *The Perfect Storm*. The results were mixed: though the film grossed a healthy $182 million at the US box office, Clooney's performance as Billy Tyne, the headstrong captain of the doomed fishing vessel *Andrea Gail*, was generally considered lacking or unremarkable.

Despite the mixed critical reception, *The Perfect Storm* served its purpose: Clooney had a mainstream box-office smash to complement the respectable critical notices for *Out of Sight* and *Three Kings*; this meant he could, for the time being, continue to pursue less aggressively commercial projects without fear of diminishing his movie-star profile. This, however, was a moot question with *O Brother, Where Art Thou?*, which was not only completed before *The Perfect Storm* hit theatres in June 2000 but was presented as a competition entry at the Cannes Film Festival in May. And though Cannes had typically received the Coens warmly if not rapturously (they had enjoyed great success at Cannes prior to 2000), the brothers' uncommonly sweet-natured musical struck a discordant note with attendees. 'You could just feel it in the room', remembers Clooney. 'Joel and Ethan and I were all sitting there in the Palais and Joel was like, "Let's get out of here! We're *done*."'[52] Covering the festival for *Entertainment Weekly*, Rebecca Ascher-Walsh noted, 'The Disney execs who paid the huge bill to give *Brother* a Cannes send-off can't be smiling this week. The picture's mixed critical reception and its no-show status at the awards ceremony points up the hazards of bringing a studio movie to Cannes – and demonstrates why Hollywood only does so in very special cases.'[53]

Ironically, the Cannes jury was in the mood for a musical that year, but they favoured the decidedly more dour tone of Lars von Trier's *Dancer in the Dark*. Meanwhile, *O Brother, Where Art Thou?* left the festival with little in

Clooney in the role of Ulysses Everett McGill in *O Brother, Where Are Thou?*, the brothers Coen's 2000 adaptation of Homer's *Odyssey*.

Following pages: Ulysses Everett McGill and his fellow escapees from a Mississippi chain gang, the irritable Pete Hogwallop (John Turturro) and the dim-witted Delmar O'Donnell (Tim Blake Nelson).

the way of acclaim or momentum for the upcoming awards season – a more precarious situation for the Coens than Clooney, given that this was their most ambitious film in terms of physical scope since their only true flop, *The Hudsucker Proxy* (1994). Unlike *Out of Sight*, no one's career was on the line if *O Brother* underperformed, but it would have certainly been disappointing for the Coens to take a commercial hit after casting a major star like Clooney. It would only serve to reinforce the notion that the Coens are at their best – not to mention most bankable – when indulging in small-scale quirks. And so their down-home *Odyssey* limped out of Cannes, looking for Ithaca in the hearts and minds of a movie-going public that had never fully understood the Coens' idiosyncratic style of storytelling.

The Smartest Idiot in the Room

This notion that *O Brother, Where Art Thou?* might be a rare misfire for Joel and Ethan Coen resonated with film critics, but meant precious little to audiences desperate for a two-hour escape from the madness of the holiday season – which was exactly where Disney⁵⁴ deposited the film on 22 December 2000. There was no subterfuge in the selling of the film; Disney embraced the vintage folk music score supervised by T Bone Burnett, and emphasized the slapstick comedy

exploits of Ulysses Everett McGill and his fellow escapees from a Mississippi chain gang, the irritable Pete Hogwallop (John Turturro) and the dim-witted Delmar O'Donnell (Tim Blake Nelson). Title notwithstanding, it is anything but the 'picture of dignity' that John Lloyd Sullivan disastrously pursued in Sturges's 1941 film; this is a wild, unabashedly silly celebration of music, malfeasance and salvation, whether it be delivered by the Lord or the begrudging forgiveness of one's family.

At the centre of this southern-fried odyssey is Clooney's less-than-noble Everett, a man who has slipped the chains of a hard labour camp in order to find and retrieve a 'treasure' of $1.2 million that he stole from an armoured car prior to his imprisonment. There's a ticking clock on this expedition – the money is buried in an area of dry land that, in four days, will be flooded by the State – and an unsettling premonition delivered by a blind man (Lee Weaver) on a pushcart, who warns the fortune they seek may not be the one they find. And there is disagreement as to which of the three fugitives is best equipped to lead the men on their madcap journey. Early on, Pete challenges Everett's unelected captaincy, to which Everett replies, 'Well, Pete, I figured it should be the one with the capacity for abstract thought.' A vote ensues: one for Pete, one for Everett; while the egoless Delmar obfuscates the decision by claiming 'I'm with you fellas.' Ultimately,

Above: Joel and Ethan Coen on the set of the film that would launch a long-running collaboration with Clooney.

Opposite: 'Say, any of you boys smithies?'

the men fall into their natural roles: Everett as know-it-all alpha dog, Pete as ticked-off tag-along and Delmar as just about the sweetest escaped convict the world has ever seen. In striking the group dynamic, Clooney recalls, 'We sort of knew right off the bat that we were idiots. But the very first day of working, Joel came over and said, "Just remember, George: you're the smartest guy in the room." When you realize you're the smartest guy in the room, that's a very different way of playing it.'[55]

Aside from his early television and film work, Clooney had yet to let out his inner imbecile in a major role, and the brain-addled brio with which he throws himself into Everett is something of a minor revelation. By 2000, audiences were largely acquainted with Clooney's penchant for self-deprecation and on-set prankishness, so it did not come as a huge surprise that the star would relish the opportunity to play the fool – especially with a pair of top-tier writer–directors feeding him a buffet line of buffoonish banter. But Everett is not a stock yokel who ignorantly dishes out homespun bromides masquerading as wisdom; he is a cheerfully erudite man of the South whose smooth elocution matches awkwardly with his slopped-on pomade (he is a 'Dapper Dan' man; 'I like the smell of my hair treatment – the pleasing odor is half the point') congealing under a ratty hairnet. Everett is a contradiction: he is an honourable man with a weakness for ill-gotten gains; he loves his wife Penny (Holly Hunter) and their seven daughters but he keeps doing wrong to do right by them, and that is why she is entertaining a 'bona fide' suitor back home while he scours the humid backwoods looking for his loot. By the time Everett recovers his treasure, Penny may already be hitched to a man with 'prospects'.

Unchained Harmony

Way back when the Coens met with Clooney on the set of *Three Kings*, they enticed him thus: 'We've got this part for you. It's about an idiot. He's about the dumbest guy you'll ever meet. We think you're perfect for it!'[56] While Clooney loved the idea, they conveniently elided the role's other challenge: Everett can sing. That this might prove challenging to the star was not something they initially considered. 'They just assumed, because my aunt was Rosemary Clooney, that I could sing', remembered Clooney. 'And I kind of assumed that I could sing. We got into the recording studio to sing "[I Am a] Man of Constant Sorrow", which is a tough song to sing. And I'd really worked on it, and I'm singing as hard as I can. Well, I finish, and I look up, and… you've got that glass booth. There's T Bone and the Coen brothers, and no one's looking up. They're just kind of like this [*looking down and gravely nodding his head*]. Already your gut just

drops out, so I walk into the room, and I go, "Eh?" And they're like, "Yeah, it's good, it's good." And they go, "Well, let's play it," hoping that I will hear it and go, "Oh, it's terrible!" I can tell already that it's going badly. So [T Bone] hits the button, and it *is* terrible. It's just terrible. But I'm not going to let them off the hook that easy, so I say, "Well, I think it's great!"'[57] Once the laughter died down, it was decided right then that bluegrass musician Dan Tyminski would provide Everett's singing voice. Joel Coen recalled, 'George has a good voice, but it's not suited to that kind of mountain music, which is hard to just walk into. You have to be brought up in it, because it's a very particular sound.'[58]

While Clooney's warbling was not quite up to snuff, he had no choice but to master Everett's Southern dialect – which, given the actor's Kentucky upbringing, was a matter of local pride. So Clooney turned to his Uncle Jack Warren, on whose tobacco farm the star had shed no shortage of sweat during his youth. '[Uncle Jack's] a pretty heavy-duty Kentucky boy. I called him up and told him that I was going to do this movie that takes place in the South. It had been a while since I'd been in Kentucky and heard the accent. So I sent my uncle the script and said, "I want you to just read the script into the tape recorder, the whole script. And then I'm going to use that. I'll get you a credit and pay you some money."'[59] The only snag regarding Warren's dialect coaching was the modest Kentuckian's unexpected inclination for minor rewriting, which caused Clooney to run afoul of the to-the-letter exactitude of the Coens. When the filmmakers confronted Clooney over his frequent dialogue substitutions, the actor, who had memorized his dialogue via Jack's tapes, immediately realized the problem: 'Uncle Jack didn't want to say "hell" or "damn".'[60] Fortunately, the Coens were forgiving and Uncle Jack still received his 'special thanks' credit at the end of the movie.

'Yes, Sir, the South is Gonna Change!'

O Brother, Where Art Thou? is by no means an accurate depiction of the 1930s Deep South; it is as much a mythical retelling of the Southern States' awkward first steps towards enlightenment (and desegregation) as the *Odyssey* is a fanciful recounting of Ulysses' return from the Trojan War. As such, the Coens adopt a visual style that combines the sepia-style photography of the era (accomplished via digital intermediate tinkering by cinematographer Roger Deakins) and powerful references to a number of iconic films from the 1920s to the late '30s. It is a haunting and ultimately hopeful evocation of the motion picture medium's power to impact the culture and change the way people view the world, and it is possible that the only movie star capable of inhabiting this throwback universe at the time

Opposite: Introducing The Soggy Bottom Boys.

Page 58: Everett faces down Penny's suitor in an effort to prove his bona fides.

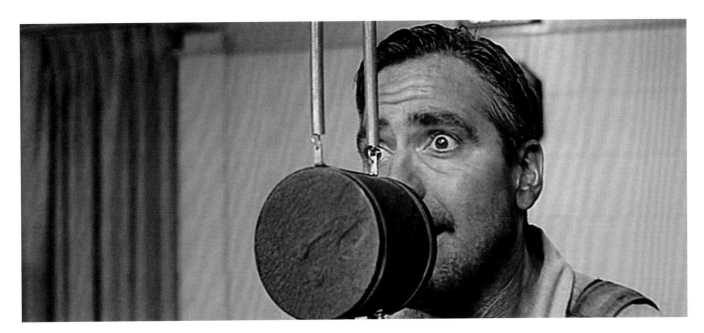

Throughout the first half of Joel and Ethan Coen's pitch-black Beltway comedy *Burn After Reading* (2008), US Marshal Harry Pfarrer (George Clooney) is up to something nefarious – at least, that is what Carter Burwell's ominously propulsive score is telling us – as he drops by Home Depot to purchase PVC tubing and various metals. Harry has been established as a squirrelly, fitness-obsessed adulterer who is sleeping with the pediatrician wife (Tilda Swinton) of a low-level CIA analyst (John Malkovich); he is a sex addict who carries around a purple sex cushion as casually as a briefcase. Given his job, and his paranoid nature, he could be a very dangerous man. So when Harry finally reveals the fruits of his clandestine labours to a personal trainer (Frances McDormand) with whom he is also having an affair, the audience is primed for something astonishing. What they get is, essentially, a rowing machine with a bobbing dildo built into the seat. Still, *Burn After Reading* was the Coens' then second-highest grossing movie in the United States and did even better business overseas. Of the several imbeciles Clooney has played for the Coens, none possesses the licentious panache of Pfarrer. And Clooney, whether he is marvelling over kitchen tiles or mulling a post-coital jog around the monuments of Washington, DC, has never allowed himself to look so pathetically vain. He is an alpha male caricature: he talks tough, but he is wound much too tightly to pose much of a threat. When he does spring into action, it is out of utter fear, and his reaction – a point-blank pistol slug to the face of Brad Pitt – is uproariously out of proportion. In an ensemble of top-tier actors playing buffoons, Clooney's Pfarrer registers as the most entertainingly, disastrously stupid of them all. It was also the completion of Clooney's 'trilogy of idiots'[g] for the Coens – or so the actor thought. According to Ethan Coen, 'The day we wrapped, he said, "All right, I've played my last idiot." So we told him it was sad that he wouldn't be working with us anymore.'[h] *Hail, Caesar!*, Clooney's fourth film with the Coens, is due out in February 2016.

Page 59: With the role of Harry Pfarrer in *Burn After Reading* (2008), Clooney embarked on a third collaboration with the Coens.

Everett momentarily resembles Clark Gable.

Opposite: Before and after the flood.

was George Clooney. Whereas his best roles to date conjured up ladykilling thoughts of Grant and Newman, Clooney this time sprouts a Clark Gable-esque moustache and does the broadest face acting of his career. His eyes go wide like an animated Chuck Jones wolf laying eyes on the most beautiful dame in the gin joint, while his forehead seems to expand several inches to a full foot depending on the degree of his surprise or outrage; his cartoonish expressions recall the rubber-faced and wild-haired antics of Nicolas Cage in the Coens' live-action Looney Tunes movie, *Raising Arizona*. This was a treacherous tightrope for Clooney to walk. 'It was definitely the scariest for me because I knew I would have to play a character', he told *The Guardian*. 'But if I was ever going to do a goofball comedy it would be with the Coen brothers. It couldn't be a Jim Carrey kind of role.'[61] If one were to judge the performance on production stills, it would be easy to assume Clooney was stuck in some low-comedic lark, but in motion it is a beautiful thing. When he sings for the first time with the Soggy Bottom Boys – a hastily thrown-together bluegrass quartet comprised of Everett, Pete, Delmar and young Tommy Johnson (Chris Thomas King) – Clooney's performance is hysterical; he is at once committed to the plaintive soul of the number and downright shocked as to where this invigoratingly anguished wail of a voice is coming from. He constantly glances around the recording

booth, looking for some manner of explanation for a musical gift he never knew he possessed. And then there is his serene enchantment upon discovering the comely Sirens washing clothes on the banks of the river: the Coens' camera pushes in on his wonderment, and the result is a shot that has been a go-to for editors of Clooney highlight reels ever since.

But Clooney's finest moment in the film – indeed, one of the most transcendent of his career – arrives at what appears to be Everett's end. Sheriff Cooley (Daniel Von Bargen) has at last caught up with the fugitives, and he aims to hang them from a sturdy tree branch right outside Everett's 'ancestral manse'. Assuming the time-honoured position of a scoundrel in his final minutes on this Earth, Everett drops to his knees and, like Renée Jeanne Falconetti in Carl Theodor Dreyer's *The Passion of Joan of Arc* (1928), pleads to God in heaven. He begs for mercy, promising to mend his ways, but what he wants more than anything is to see his daughters again. Everett's prayer is answered by the flood promised in the first act of the film; Pete and Delmar believe it is a miracle but Everett knows better. And yet Everett appears to be a changed man in the film's final scene. He may present Penny with the wrong wedding ring, but he is the picture of contentment as he strolls through town with his wife and daughters. This, in itself, is a miracle.

Revival

Whereas Everett was saved by the divine power of man-made flooding, *O Brother, Where Art Thou?* was rescued by good old-fashioned word of mouth, with many critics singling out Clooney's masterfully stylized turn. In a full-throated rave for *The New York Times*, A.O. Scott observed, 'Mr. Clooney not only looks like Clark Gable, with his hair slicked against his scalp and his carefully etched Art Deco mustache, but he also gives the kind of detached, matinee-idol performance that used to be Gable's trademark.'[62] But it was not the critics who lit the fuse on *O Brother*'s mainstream explosion; the primary draw was the music, which powered the film's original soundtrack LP to five million copies sold and five Grammys (including Album of the Year). The movie would stand as the Coens' highest grossing picture until 2007's *No Country for Old Men* and, most importantly, gave Clooney greater commercial clout in terms of carrying riskier studio fare. Clooney won a Golden Globe for the Best Performance by an Actor in a Motion Picture – Comedy or Musical – and beat out the formidable likes of Robert De Niro, Jim Carrey and Mel Gibson. True, it was just the Golden Globes, but it was his first major recognition as a film *actor* not just a movie star. The award also offered final validation that Clooney was not just a charismatic TV performer moonlighting

in movies. Ulysses Everett McGill was a pitch straight to Clooney's wheelhouse, and he swatted it into the cheap seats. The combination of clowning and deep, staring-death-in-the-face pathos proved an ideal mixture for Clooney: it wedded his self-deprecating personality with his carefully meted-out sincerity. He may not have been able to sing in the manner required by the role, but he hit every note in the script with absolute clarity. Clooney may never again find another role so perfectly suited to his instrument – save for his next part, which would *intentionally* lean more heavily on his movie star persona than any film he had done before.

Above: Ulysses returns to his wife (Holly Hunter) and daughters after his long journey.

Opposite: A man of constant, cartoonish range: Clooney's broad array of expressions in *O Brother*.

4

Danny Ocean

Ocean's Eleven (2001)
Steven Soderbergh

'Does he make you laugh?'
'He doesn't make me cry.'
—Danny Ocean / Tess Ocean

After the box-office windfall of *The Perfect Storm* and the surprise critical/commercial success of *O Brother, Where Art Thou?*, Clooney had at last reached that plateau of personal creative freedom he had yearned for since the embarrassment of *Batman & Robin*. He would turn forty on 6 May 2001, so he was acutely aware that this was the time to get serious about his ambitions as a producer and director, which had thus far sputtered in his Maysville Pictures partnership with Robert Lawrence. Clooney and Lawrence founded the company in 1997 (with offices at Clooney's home base of Warner Bros.), eager to churn out, as Lawrence told *Variety*, a series of 'thinking-man's, character-driven action-thrillers'.[63] The endeavour had a wisp of a personal touch, given its moniker's reference to the Clooney homestead in Maysville, Kentucky, but the duo differed on development philosophy. When Maysville's deal was up in the fall of 1999, Clooney and Lawrence amicably went their separate ways.

Despite Maysville's failure, Warner Bros. had every intention of maintaining their business relationship with Clooney – he was a home-grown star and they wanted to reap the rewards of their unswerving faith in his burgeoning career. Though the feeling was mutual, Clooney needed to find a partner who shared his desire for quality over quantity – a notion that was generally anathema to studio lot producers. The solution was obvious to Clooney's assistant, Amy Cohen: Soderbergh. Clooney and his *Out of Sight* director promptly got together for dinner and thus, in 2000, Section Eight Productions was born.

The Recalibration of Cool

When Frank Sinatra passed away, in 1998, he took with him an inimitable combination of cocktail-swilling swagger, impeccably phrased crooning and on-screen surliness – all of which carefully played into or off of his public persona. Few performers have more gracefully transitioned from recording star to matinee idol *and*, ultimately, award-winning actor as Sinatra – but his career is

less a blueprint to success than the fairytale version. By the late 1950s, he was the sun around which the biggest names in entertainment orbited; with his Rat Pack (an ever-rotating coterie of celebrities that primarily featured Dean Martin, Sammy Davis, Jr, Peter Lawford and Joey Bishop), he exuded an impossible kind of cool that, if attempted by anyone else, would have drawn howls of derisive laughter. And depending on whom you ask, that era – most indelibly preserved on film in all-star goofs such as *Ocean's 11* (1960), *Sergeants 3* (1962) and *Robin and the 7 Hoods* (1964) – is either a warm blanket of Kennedy-era nostalgia or unbearably smug. It is arguable as to whether any of the Rat Pack films have aged well, but many cinephiles will stick up for the widescreen pleasures of Lewis Milestone's *Ocean's 11*: it is slick, silly and moderately interested in giving the audience a good time out at the movies. Just do not ask Clooney to defend it.

'My friends and I are on a bus going cross country', recalls Clooney. 'I get the tape for *Ocean's 11*, figuring it's the coolest guys in the world, Frank, Sammy, Dean. We pop it in, and it's like, "Yeah, woooo, *Ocean's 11*!" Ten minutes in, and it's like, "Woo!" Another five minutes, it's like, "Whoa, get this off." *Ocean's 11* isn't a good movie at all.'[64] Even those who adore the film would likely concede that it is more valuable as a time capsule than a crackerjack heist film; regardless, it is not exactly the type of movie that would rank high on a studio's remake queue, and certainly not as a potential big-screen reunion for Clooney and A-list auteur Soderbergh (who had just won the Best Director Oscar for *Traffic*).

'Then Warner Bros. sent me Ted Griffin's remake script, and I said, "Wow, this is a great script"', said Clooney. 'The only thing similar is eleven guys pulling a heist. I'm not playing Frank Sinatra, nobody's playing Sammy or Dean. Steven calls me that night and says, "I just finished *Ocean's Eleven*, and I know how to do it." I've known Steven for four years and I've sent him twenty scripts, and he not only passes, he says, "No way, dude." He's a snob.'[65] But the Griffin screenplay attacked the concept as a caper comedy first and a working vacation for the actors second. 'If there's a germ of an idea that just got pollinated in the wrong way, you can remake

Clooney plays the smooth criminal Danny Ocean in Steven Soderbergh's *Ocean's Eleven* (2001).

65

Opposite: Just released from prison, Danny Ocean dives back into a life of crime.

A scene from *Ocean's 11* (1960) by Lewis Milestone starring Dean Martin (as Sam Harmon), Peter Lawford (as Jimmy Foster), Henry Silva (as Roger Corneal), Buddy Lester (as Vince Massler), Sammy Davis, Jr (as Josh Howard), Joey Bishop (as 'Mushy' O'Connors) and Frank Sinatra (as Danny Ocean).

Following pages: Ocean and his partner-in-crime Rusty Ryan (Brad Pitt) exposing their project to Reuben Tishkoff (Elliott Gould).

a not-very-good film', said Clooney. 'The only way to do it was like *Murder on the Orient Express*, [or] those old Irwin Allen films, pack it full of stars but do it in a funny way.'[66] So Clooney and Soderbergh immediately booked a meeting with executive Lorenzo di Bonaventura at Warner Bros., got probably one of the easiest green lights in motion-picture history and began assembling their dream cast. 'We start talking to Brad Pitt and he's in', said Clooney. 'Steven had just finished *Erin Brockovich* with Julia Roberts, and he sends her the script with $20 tucked in and a note saying, "I hear you get twenty a picture now." She's in. Then everybody starts calling, you can't imagine the names. We're going to have a terrific cast, everybody working below rate. We said, "If we all get paid, we can't make the movie, so why don't we all just take a big chunk of the backend, work cheap and see if there's any money at the end."'[67]

All-Star Robbery

In citing 'those old Irwin Allen films' as models of all-star extravaganzas done right, Clooney was either being mildly facetious or acknowledging a predilection for a type of gaudy entertainment that is not all that different from the original *Ocean's 11*. Allen's movies (e.g. *The Poseidon Adventure*, *The Towering Inferno* and *The Swarm*) generally centred on a specific crisis – capsized luxury liner, burning skyscraper, killer bees – conquered in some manner by the principal cast; but there were also big-name stars who turned up solely to fill out dead-end 'b' and 'c' stories that concluded in their touching/tragic/spectacular demise. Soderbergh, however, is not a filmmaker who indulges such nonsense; if he is going to make an epic, he is going to get it as streamlined as possible, retaining only the most essential elements. One might argue that paring down the wretched excess of star-studded parties masquerading as feature films defeats the point of mounting them, but celebrity in 2001 was not the far-off, fantasy-land ideal that it was in the 1960s and '70s. In less than a decade the internet had greatly reduced the size of the world; famous people seemed more tangible than ever (a sense that would only be enhanced by the advent of social media in a few short years). The novelty of seeing Clooney, Brad Pitt, Julia Roberts et al. on screen together for an entire movie would wear off quickly; this sucker needed to cook.

Soderbergh, however, opted for more of a simmer building to a controlled boil. The film begins in an unassuming manner, with Clooney's Danny Ocean being released from prison. Clad in a light green jump suit and with a grizzled beard, Danny still looks like a million bucks – but a few moments later he is cleanly shaved, dazzlingly coiffed and exuding a bank-breaking charm somewhere north of ten figures. He is

dressed to steal, which is precisely the plan; upon taking his first breath of free air, he is off to Los Angeles – in violation of his parole – to seduce his old partner-in-crime, Rusty Ryan (Brad Pitt), back into the illicit highlife. Ocean's plan is preposterous: knock off three of Las Vegas's most prominent casinos (The Mirage, The Bellagio and The MGM Grand) on the night of a heavily anticipated (i.e. wagered upon) heavyweight boxing match. To accomplish this impossible task, the pair go about recruiting a murderer's row of thieves, conmen, mechanics and one demolition expert (Don Cheadle sporting a Cockney accent that he swears is not intentionally awful). Their play is backed by Reuben Tishkoff (Elliott Gould), an out-to-pasture former casino owner who would enjoy a measure of revenge against Terry Benedict (Andy Garcia), his rival and owner of all three targeted establishments. It is also personal for Danny, whose ex-wife, Tess (Julia Roberts), is now married to the venal and vindictive Benedict.

The stakes are high, considering the amount of money targeted by Ocean's crew ($160 million) as well as the discomfiting fact that no one has ever successfully hit one Vegas casino let alone three (a history amusingly recounted by Carl Reiner's elderly confidence man Saul Bloom), but it is really the fate of Danny's pride that matters to the viewer. Like Clooney, he is an overwhelmingly charismatic bachelor whose indiscretions – ripping off rich people – seem excusable, if not charming. This crooked virtue mirrors Clooney's own penchant for taking on perceived frauds or jerks who abuse power. 'He's absolutely allergic to pretension', says Soderbergh. 'He also sees red when he's confronted with unearned or irrational authority. He's one of the few people I know who picks on people that are bigger than him – in the philosophical sense. He goes after people like Bill O'Reilly, and that guy's got a gigantic microphone.[68] George does not back down, period. If he feels strongly about something, he'll go after anybody – as opposed to other people in the business who *always* pick on people who are smaller than them. I think that quality comes across. I'm sure there's been instances of actors who've played characters with some sort of code or set of principals or level of sincerity that turns out to be complete horseshit, but in George's case I think that quality really does come across.'[69]

This is also key to Ocean's likeability. He is an honourable scoundrel up against a backstabbing billionaire who collects people like they are trophies. On a certain level, the viewer's rooting interest is, as in the 2000 US Presidential Election, determined by who one would rather have a beer with. And while Garcia is probably delightful company in real life, Clooney's reputation for gaiety and kindness is just too powerful to resist. It is a testament to Clooney's dominance of the movie that, when the crew assembles for

a strangely moving curtain call at The Bellagio's fountain (dreamily scored to Debussy's 'Clair de lune'), Danny's absence is palpably felt.

Clever Pleasure

One of *Ocean's Eleven*'s most sublime qualities is the cast's evident lack of ego. Though Soderbergh confesses that the films are a bit of a nightmare directorially (primarily due to the challenge of shooting eleven people in one room), he was pleased to find that his actors could not stay away from the set – especially Clooney. But for the cast they are a blast. And George never leaves the set anyway. I asked him about that during *Out of Sight*. I was like, '"You never leave the set." He said, "I've been trying to get here my whole life. Why would I get here, and not want to be here?" I thought, "That's exactly right."'[70]

Clooney is visibly more relaxed in this movie than he had been in anything since *Out of Sight*; in fact, his performance is really just a low-key variation on Jack Foley. Ocean is a little more suave, but only as a means of keeping up appearances as he interacts with high society. Even then, Clooney still manages to trot out his dorky 'Frankenstein walk', the origins of which still baffle Soderbergh: 'It's this kind of wide-stanced thing, which is funny because that's not the way he walks at all.'[71] When it comes to striking a sexual spark with Roberts's Tess (over a dinner to which he has not been invited), Danny opts for low-key contrition that gradually crescendos to the air of self-satisfied confidence that both attracted and repelled his ex-wife. He cannot imagine Tess is at all happy with the overtly corrupt Benedict; worse, his pride is wounded that she would prefer to stay by Benedict's side even if Danny were to miraculously establish himself as the better option. He appeals to her sense of play: 'Does he make you laugh?' Tess's curt reply: 'He doesn't make me cry.' It is a brutal kiss-off that denies Danny the one quality that might win her back; after some tense, tough-guy banter with Benedict, Danny leaves the restaurant with his tail firmly tucked between his legs. Though the stakes are not terribly high (there is not much doubt that Danny will pull off the heist and, if nothing else, take down Benedict), the sight of Clooney's charm offensive failing is slightly disconcerting.

Ocean's Eleven is an utterly ephemeral film, but it clings to one's memory because its pleasures are so unassumingly clever. Aside from the crowd-pleasing sight gag of a monster truck running over its miniature, remote-controlled doppelgänger, the comedy is largely verbal and casually delivered. It is a variety show of sorts put on by a troupe of performers who know the difference between effortlessness and disengaged. The tone is set early by Clooney and Pitt, who banter at a Hollywood hot spot while young

Opposite: Danny crashes dinner with Tess (Julia Roberts) and Terry Benedict (Andy Garcia).

Following pages: Danny paid his debt to society but not to Tess.

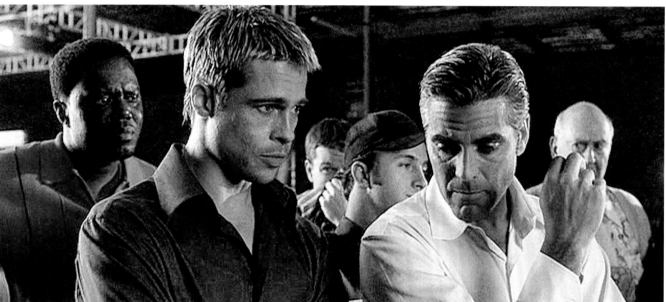

Opposite: Danny and the gang gather around demolition man Basher Tarr (Don Cheadle).

Above: Soderbergh goes handheld, to Clooney's amusement.

revellers – including up-and-coming actors playing themselves – flit in and around them; the joke here is that Clooney and Pitt are the lame old guys at the club. In any other world, they would be mobbed by beautiful women; in this reality, they just want to go home. This is in marked contrast to the original *Ocean's 11*, where Sinatra and his Rat Pack dine out for two hours on the misguided notion that the audience will consider their very presence entertainment enough. Clooney and his crew are not that conceited; they strike a friendly, inclusive vibe and stick to it to the denouement. This is Clooney's way of inviting everyone to the party, and he would be devastated if his guests did not have a fabulous time.

The Big Score

To the surprise of no one, *Ocean's Eleven* opened to terrific business on 7 December 2001. By the end of the weekend it had taken in $38 million at the US box office, on its way to $450 million worldwide. Had the cast taken their full quote salary, the movie would have never turned a profit, but at a reported $85 million, it was a big enough hit that two more entries in the series seemed to Warner Bros. like a sound financial decision. Critically, *Ocean's Eleven* was greeted warmly, if not ecstatically, with Clooney drawing raves for capably anchoring the ship. Writing for

Salon, Stephanie Zacharek observed, 'George Clooney, as smoothie thief Daniel Ocean, is a movie star in every sense of the word. He carries the picture in his breast pocket: You look for his face when you feel the plot getting a little too busy or too slick.'[72] Elvis Mitchell of *The New York Times* found Clooney's variation on a theme originated by Sinatra a far more pleasing rendition: 'Mr. Clooney, the logical heir to Sinatra's private-jet charm, portrays Danny Ocean, Chairman of the Bored. Sinatra, who played Ocean the first time around, may have been the first jazz actor, but he never showed the attention span to go with the talent. Mr. Clooney does. His line readings are choice: he never raises his voice, which is all velvet arrogance with a minimum of fuss.'[73]

Though *Ocean's Eleven* was practically a guaranteed success the day Warner Bros. signed off on it, the project was still a risk in terms of image – particularly for Clooney. Here was Hollywood's throwback heir to the classic movie-star throne, a man beginning to associate himself with A-plus filmmaking, spending his audience goodwill on a homage to a fame-fuelled folly. Sure, he had earned great critical acclaim for *Out of Sight*, *Three Kings* and *O Brother, Where Art Thou?*, but this was, on the surface, the type of lark that seemed beneath Clooney (and, for that matter, Soderbergh). This could have easily been viewed as a premature victory lap. And yet the

Baby I'm (Something Like) a Star

A fellow can only be dubbed the 'next Cary Grant' for so long before someone takes a whack at this low-hanging, blasphemous fruit. For example, writing for *The Wrap* in 2009, Naomi Serviss lazily observed, 'What happened to real film stars with real faces? I'm talking Cary Grant caliber, who brought not only *savoir faire* to film, but had that "It" factor that ruled Tinseltown, especially in the late, great '30s.'[i] Yes! That 'It' factor! The ineffable quality that remains undefined because it exists only in the collective conscious of moviegoers – the folks who truly decide who and what possesses 'It'. Serviss never got around to answering her own question, probably because it is silly to suggest George Clooney is not a 'real star' with a 'real face' (just ask that Academy of Plastic Surgeons!). But if it is a question of what constitutes a star in an age of social media, Clooney himself has an interesting take on the quandary: 'In all fairness, if you think about movie stars, they don't really exist anymore. They sort of stopped because of television. Movie stars like Clark Gable, Spencer Tracy and Bogart basically played themselves in all those movies. We knew them as that. There was Laurence Olivier who played a lot of characters, but we didn't take to him as much as we took to Spencer Tracy or Clark Gable, Cary Grant or Gregory Peck. In a way, we're able to break out from that a little bit more. The unfortunate thing is I think you're demystified because they know more about your life because there are so many outlets. But in a way, you're sort of set free because there's always going to be an awful lot of celebrities out there… that haven't done anything and are famous. That creates a vacuum, in a way.'[j] Strangely, Steven Soderbergh sees Clooney's onscreen persona as more British in its construction: 'He has… almost what I would call this English approach to performance in that he would never dream of burdening you with his process. I find a lot of Brits are like that. They pride themselves in that they can turn it on, and they can turn it off. I happen to know he thinks about this stuff a lot…, but he finds it not really helpful to burden the director with what you're trying to find on your own.'[k] In other words, he keeps the inner workings of his craft, and the projection of his image, to himself. Clooney has 'It', and he protects 'It'.

Opposite: Attending the
première of Tony Gilroy's
Michael Clayton (2007),
during the Venice Festival
in August 2007.

Third and final film
of Soderbergh series,
Ocean's Thirteen (2007).

across-the-board acceptance, if not enjoyment,
of *Ocean's Eleven* was the ultimate vindication
of Clooney's movie-star stature. On the surface,
the film is nothing more than a glitzy heist film;
they have been done bigger and better. But the
opportunity to hang out with Clooney and his
pals was sufficient justification for the price of
admission. It was not a spot-the-famous-people
spectacle like *The Cannonball Run* (1981); it was
a strangely conscientious blockbuster. It is like
watching a professional sports All-Star Game
where the athletes play a little defence and make
it a game. The subsequent *Ocean's* films got away
from this a little, venturing into self-referential
territory or self-indulgence (the closing poker
scene in *Twelve* makes the audience feel like they
are on the other side of the velvet ropes, craning
their necks to get a look inside the club). But this
movie got it right. It was Clooney bringing the
party to his fans, with his fans stumbling out of
the theatre on a Champagne high, feeling elated
that this guy is the genuine article.

5

Chris Kelvin

Solaris (2002)
Steven Soderbergh

'Everything we've done is forgiven.'
—Rheya Kelvin

Before forming Section Eight with Clooney, Soderbergh was asked by a friend if he had ever liked to make a science-fiction film: 'I said, "Well, I don't know, because I feel since *Star Wars* they've tilted pretty far into the action genre and I'm not really interested in technology or gadgets." And she said, "Give me an example of the kind of science-fiction film that you like." I said, "*Solaris*."'[74] His friend looked into the rights to both Stanisław Lem's 1961 novel and Andrei Tarkovsky's 1972 film, and learned that all the material had just been acquired by filmmaker James Cameron. Intrigued, Soderbergh met with the *Titanic* director, and pitched his idea, which was entirely different from Cameron's concept. 'What I would've done would've been more like *The Abyss*,' said Cameron, 'where visual set pieces might have gotten in the way of what is a clean line as a relationship film… [Soderbergh's] not interested in the hardware or the visual effects very much, which is good.'[75]

Pleased with Soderbergh's take on the project, Cameron handed over the reins to the movie, with scripting beginning at some point during the editing of *Traffic*. It was to be a more cerebral and erotic envisioning of Lem's novel, akin, in Soderbergh's words, to a collision of *2001* and *Last Tango in Paris*. 'The fact is you could make five different movies out of that book', said Soderbergh. 'It's kind of a tree with huge branches that go in a lot of different directions, and I took one of those and ran in one direction.'[76] He was also running toward one particular actor for the lead role of Chris Kelvin, the psychiatrist sent to check in on the troubled crew of a space station orbiting the titular planet, and that actor was *not* Soderbergh's good friend and Section Eight Productions partner George Clooney. 'I'd made tentative attempts to reach out to Daniel Day-Lewis', said Soderbergh, 'But he wasn't in a working mode at that point.'[77] So the inveterate letter-writer Clooney took pen to paper and fired off one of his famous missives to his filmmaking pal. 'I knew Steven was talking to another actor', said Clooney. 'I'd read the *Solaris* script and I was really turned on by the idea of it, but I also didn't want to put Steven in a stressful position. He is

my friend and my partner. So I thought the best way to give him the out was for me to give him some space by writing and say, "Look, I'd love to take a shot at it."'[78] For an actor who thrives on challenges and loathes complacency, *Solaris* was an opportunity for Clooney to slice himself open and bear his soul; he would be tasked with carrying a film on his ability to convey grief. Every second of his screen time would require Clooney to work a completely different set of performance muscles, which had to be as exciting as it was frightening.

Clooney's *modus operandi* of valuing script quality over a project's commercial potential had been paying off nicely over the last two years: his last three films were hits or full-scale blockbusters. Having at last passed the age of forty, the time for making his mark was upon him, and he was forging ahead with what are, to this date, two of the riskiest movies he has ever made: *Confessions of a Dangerous Mind* (2002, his feature directing début) and *Solaris*. That he was tackling both in such close proximity to each other – *Solaris* would begin principal photography as soon as *Confessions of a Dangerous Mind* wrapped – would test his creative resolve. Making movies is strenuous business; to then turn around and attempt one of the most emotionally demanding roles of one's career was a feat of hubristic potential. But Clooney could not let *Solaris* go.

'I'm full of grief and confusion myself', said Clooney to an audience at London's National Film Theatre.[79] After once again emphasizing the importance of starting with a great screenplay, Clooney, thinking more as a producer than at any point in his career thus far, expanded on the notion of risk-taking that would define his career: 'You feel like it's a really uncompromising film that's got to be done within a studio. We've been trying to push our involvement within the studio system, sort of push the things that we've learned from foreign and independent films through the '80s and push those things back into the studio system. Like *Out of Sight* isn't your standard studio film by any means; *Three Kings* wasn't the standard Warner Bros. kind of film. And this one seemed like it was really going to push it. And I liked the idea that Steven was raising a lot of questions that he was trying to work out himself, and I thought it would really be fun to go on that

For his third collaboration with director Steven Soderbergh, Clooney plays the role of Chris Kelvin in *Solaris* (2002).

Following pages: Psychiatrist Chris Kelvin makes a troubling discovery aboard Solaris station.

79

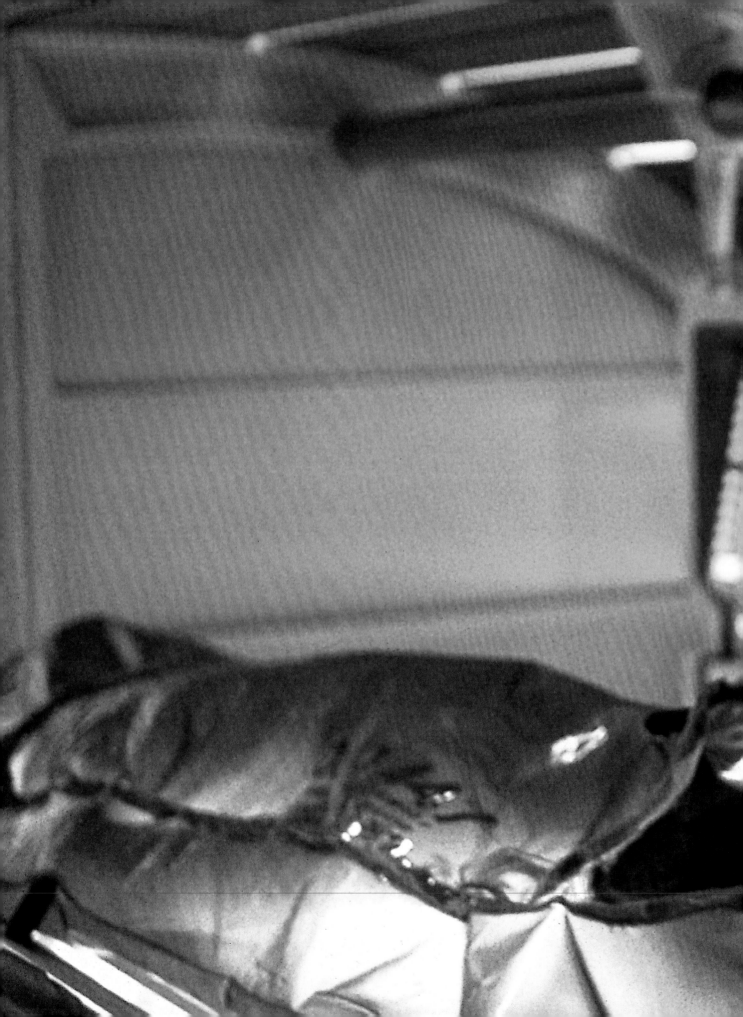

Opposite, top: Kelvin assesses the state of Solaris station.

Opposite, bottom: Kelvin with Gordon (Viola Davis), one of the last remaining crew of the space station orbiting the planet Solaris.

Once on Solaris, Kelvin is also visited by his wife, Rheya (Natascha McElhone), who committed suicide back on Earth.

Following pages: The more time he spends with Rheya, the more Kelvin becomes reattached.

run with him.'[80] Then came a dig – presumably, at his *Three Kings* director: 'You can trust a director like Steven with that kind of risk – I wouldn't have done this with some directors, who shall remain nameless.'[81]

Off into the Cosmos

Lem's novel is a terse yet philosophically dense tale of space explorers who, while studying the planet Solaris from orbit, come into contact with 'visitors', which are fresh manifestations of subconscious tumult and suppressed grief spawned by the sentient planet for unknown reasons. Soderbergh's script generally sticks to the basic plot details of Lem's novel: Snow (Jeremy Davies) has been visited by his brother, while the ship's commander, Gibarian (Ulrich Tukur) – who killed himself before Kelvin's (George Clooney) arrival – was reacquainted with his deceased son. While Kelvin is attempting to make sense of these intergalactic hauntings ('I could tell you what's happening,' offers Snow, 'but I don't know if it would really tell you what's happening'), he is confronted with his own 'visitor': his wife Rheya (Natascha McElhone), who committed suicide back on Earth. Upon her first appearance, a spooked Kelvin jettisons her off in a space capsule rather than deal with what, to his rigidly logical mind, cannot possibly be; however, when she turns up again the next day, he recognizes that,

no matter how improbable, she is real. But he does not take this opportunity to plumb the depths of their tragically failed relationship; instead, the minute she displays symptoms of the apparent mental illness that plagued her back on Earth, Kelvin, viewing her as an impediment to dealing with the pressing issues of the mission's status, simply begins medicating her as he attempts to communicate with the station's other inhabitant, the reclusive and accusatory Gordon (Viola Davis), so that he can return home. However, the more time he spends with Rheya, the more Kelvin becomes reattached, falling in love with her all over again, which creates acrimony when Gordon finally re-emerges from her solitude with a tangible, and quite final, solution to the problem of the visitors, provoking arguments over the intent of the planet and whether it is pernicious or benevolent.

Soderbergh's previously stated disinterest in hard science fiction led him to abandon Lem's long passages on the history of 'Solaristics' and the heightened, ultimately-incomprehensible-to-the-human-mind communication being attempted by the planet's homeostatic ocean (again, the manifestations are not hallucinations; they are quite real). Instead, he throws a microscope on the sexually and emotionally charged relationship shared by Kelvin and Rheya on Earth, meting out the details of their romance in flashback and present-day exchanges on the ship. The movie is

an unburdening – for its characters, for its director and for its actors. Nothing this emotionally raw can be faked; Soderbergh creates a melancholy, rainy-day mood from the outset, with an evocative shot of a window being pelted with rain, and lets this pensiveness seep into his performers. As Kelvin and Rheya come together and apart, and together and apart again, there is a constant foreboding, a realization that their time together is destined to end tragically. What matters to Soderbergh is that Kelvin makes some kind of peace with this; regardless of his role in Rheya's downward mental spiral (he left her upon learning she had an abortion without telling him), there is – in some manner of the word, in some plane of existence – forgiveness.

Riddle Box

Principal photography on *Confessions of a Dangerous Mind* proved more wearying than Clooney had expected, which he allows might have been the proper state of mind with which to approach Kelvin. 'I'd set up an editing bay at Warner Bros. and I was literally shooting on the set for 13–14 hours a day and then editing for three to four hours a night and sleeping in the trailer lot. And I thought that it would work to my advantage, the fact that I was physically tired.'[82] It shows. Clooney's fatigue dulls his inherent playfulness, rendering him not just still, but sombre. The viewer knows right away that Kelvin is a man hauling around several psychic tons of anguish, which gives Clooney a much-needed head start to projecting a kind of vulnerability he had only hinted at in previous roles. 'All you really do is show up on the set and try not to have any of those barriers, or those crutches that actors have. And with this, there were none of those crutches – there weren't that many other actors, there was no humour in it, there aren't things that you can usually hide behind. And you just show up and let Steven say, "Okay, it's the last 13 seconds of your life – go." And trust him when he says, "Okay, now 20% more existential grief"… So again it comes down to trust.'[83]

This being their third collaboration, Soderbergh was used to Clooney's unfussy, ready-to-roll style of acting. But *Solaris* was a different animal altogether: it was not just another case of modulating charisma and jocularity; Clooney had to look like a man confronted by the nearness of death and the agonizing experience of losing the love of his life all over again. Soderbergh's insistence on long takes removed the safety net of coverage; Clooney would have to do this all in one. 'The level of vulnerability that role required was something he hadn't been asked to portray', says Soderbergh. 'I think that's why he wanted to do it. He felt like, "I can do it, and I want to do it."'[84] Getting there took more effort than normal. 'One of the scenes that we

really worked on hard', says Soderbergh, 'was the scene where he wakes up and she's there for the first time. First, he thinks that he dreamt it, then he looks and she's still there. This is really hard stuff to pull off. I do recall him going, "Let me try that again." You're really threading a needle. You're trying to exhibit real behavior in a circumstance that is totally unreal. I know that we were both anxious that we would get it right.'[85] And yet Soderbergh is adamant that the extra workload never took a toll on Clooney. 'If anything, it was nice', he says. 'He was kind of raw. Not in a bad way, but defenseless.'[86]

Soderbergh might have found Clooney a little less 'on' during the shoot, but McElhone remembers George being George. 'There's a very relaxing environment that Steven manages to create on a film set, however nervous he says he was in hindsight. And George contributes to that, because he never takes anything seriously. He's always fooling around and making everyone laugh and putting everyone before himself, which is quite unactorly and certainly very unstarry. What can I say? I can only get mushy and embarrassing and that's very un-English, so we'll just leave it at that.'[87]

The on-screen dynamic between Clooney and McElhone is a unique one in that it requires the suave leading man to be the quarry. From their first encounter on a train, it is almost a dare: Rheya sits across from Kelvin, practically flush, draped in an emerald green jacket and brandishing a doorknob. They wind up together at the same party, where the eye contact is off-the-charts hot; a coupling seems to be a *fait accompli*, but Rheya is going to make him work for it. Their first exchange is a skilful flirtation, with Rheya knocking Kelvin back on his heels with her first utterance. Can Kelvin keep up?

Rheya: Don't blow it.
Kelvin: [*laughs*] You start.
Rheya: I did.
Kelvin: Really? Alright. I'm going to resist the impulse to ask you about the doorknob.
Rheya: Do you always resist your impulses?
Kelvin: Not always.
Rheya: Try poetry.
Kelvin: 'And death shall have no dominion.'
Rheya: Hm, Thomas. It's not a very happy poem, though.
Kelvin: Well, you didn't seem very happy when I saw you on the train.
Rheya: [*laughs*] I wasn't.
Kelvin: And tonight?
Rheya: It's early.

'We auditioned a few people', says Soderbergh. 'I had George in the room with a few people because I knew it was really crucial. Natascha was someone I really liked, and he did, too. The camera *really* likes her.'[88] Their sex scenes together, which required both to be filmed naked, are the most sensual Clooney has shot outside of his

Top: Kelvin, Snow (Jeremy Davies) and Gordon observe Rheya.

Bottom: Kelvin's mental state begins to deteriorate.

Following pages: Kelvin is besieged by the 'cruel miracles' of Solaris.

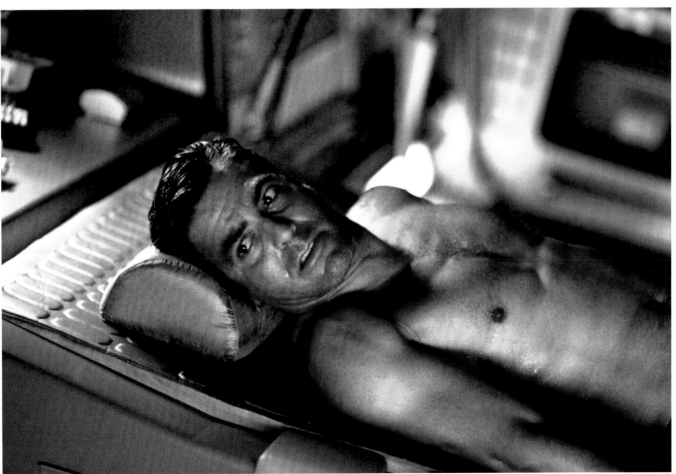

tango with Jennifer Lopez in *Out of Sight*. That scene, however, is playful; this is raw, carnal and – in keeping with the pathologies of both characters – desperate. They cannot see ahead to the tragic end, but the viewer, aided by Soderbergh's non-linear editing, knows it is coming. On an historical note, this was Clooney's first official nude scene, which, according to Soderbergh, was hardly epochal. 'It wasn't a big deal. I was fairly straightforward with what I needed. You send everyone away, and I'm the camera operator. It wasn't as traumatic as it might have been. In most cases, they don't eat for the week prior.'[89] Clooney's take on baring his posterior for the camera: 'I wanted to be nude in front of Steven.'[90]

Solaris, We Have a Problem

As a remake of a beloved, if difficult to penetrate, science-fiction film, *Solaris* was never going to be an easy sell to critics or audiences. Producer James Cameron realized this before the film was even finished. 'I remember when we were doing it', Cameron said, '"You know, in ten years people are going to like this a lot." If you could've seen the faces of the people at 20th Century Fox, it was priceless.'[91] The $47 million film was lightly marketed, but received a wide, 2,406-screen release; it was not exactly what is considered a 'dump' in industry terms, but it certainly was not

sold with confidence. Moreover, moviegoers are often conscious of when a studio is uncertain about a film, and they stayed far away: *Solaris* grossed a grant total of $30 million worldwide, and received a dreaded 'F' from the audience polling company CinemaScore.

The film received a majority of positive reviews, but many critics were put off by what they perceived as a lack of feeling on Soderbergh's part; they held that it was too sleek and under-emoted for its own good. To back up this assertion, a few focused their ire squarely on the playing-against-type movie star. Writing for *Entertainment Weekly*, Owen Gleiberman said, 'McElhone is certainly someone to pine for – there are depths to her apple-cheeked sculptural beauty – but Clooney may be too swank an actor to suffer this moodily. He is, rather, the perfect poster idol for a film that serves up romantic tragedy as stylishly cryptic solemnity chic.'[92] But for the most part, even those who could not connect with Soderbergh's film felt Clooney had turned in one of his strongest performances. *Variety* critic Todd McCarthy observed, 'Clooney does a highly creditable job of carrying the film's freight on his shoulders even as the cargo becomes increasingly unwieldy.'[93] Chiming in with one of the most enthusiastic reviews, Roger Ebert was hugely impressed with Clooney's work. 'Clooney has successfully survived being named *People Magazine*'s sexiest man alive by deliberately

Above: With Steven Soderbergh, on the set of the film.

Opposite: Todd Haynes' *Far from Heaven* (2002) is one of Section Eight's most celebrated productions.

When George Clooney and Steven Soderbergh founded Section Eight Productions, they had visions of championing movies outside of the current mainstream, while supporting talented filmmakers who often have to scramble for financing. Discussing the company's philosophy with *The New York Times*, Clooney said, 'My motivation is not to make money which, on occasion, makes us a sorry proposition. I think you could make an argument that it is not important to have too much taste as a producer if you are working for a large company. It's hard to find commercial stuff that doesn't make you feel bad in the morning.'[l] Warner Bros. encouraged the venture by giving the company Jack Warner's spacious former office, and the studio did its part by enthusiastically backing such non-commercial films as *Syriana* and *Michael Clayton*. Did Section Eight produce any true classics? Convincing cases can certainly be made for Todd Haynes's *Far from Heaven* (2002), Clooney's *Good Night, and Good Luck* (2005)

and Tony Gilroy's *Michael Clayton* (2007). That's three out of twenty-two – three more classics than most studio-bound production companies turn out in their entire lifespan. According to Soderbergh, the company's undoing was its success: 'The workload became untenable. We had so many things going that it was starting to pull away from our day jobs, and both of us felt it. We had said from the beginning, "If we can keep this lean and mean, and it's fun, we'll keep doing it." And it became that thing where there was so much going on, in order for it to survive it would have to expand. At the end of the day, it's me and George. We have to see everything. We have to look at everything. If somebody's got a problem, they have to call us. We are the company. When you have that level of responsibility on that many movies, and you're trying to make your own movie, something's got to give. So halfway through the contract, we both had a conversation where, "This is too much work." And producing's terrible. You've really got

to have a certain DNA to do it. It's problems. Every call is a problem.'[m]

In the summer of 2006, Clooney and Soderbergh quietly announced the closure of Section Eight. Though there were still films in their production pipeline, Clooney wasted no time in announcing his new venture, Smoke House Pictures. Teaming with his long-time friend and *Good Night, and Good Luck* co-writer Grant Heslov, Clooney promised more of the high-aiming, adult-skewing same from the new company. In an interview with *The Hollywood Reporter*, Clooney explained, 'We'd like to keep it along the same vision, which is to try to infuse the things that we've learned over the years from independent and foreign films into the studio system because they have the best resources. That's the same sort of philosophy that Steven and I had with Section Eight. Grant is a great friend, a talented producer, was a great executive and producer for Steven and I, and a good writer. We'd like to carry on that same tradition, and we like the idea of starting it clean again.'[n] The first official Smoke House release would be *Leatherheads*, the long-in-development account of a 1920s professional football team that had once been set up for Soderbergh to direct. The film was now a directing-and-starring assignment for Clooney, and was scheduled for release in December 2007 (finally released in March 2008).

Above: Kelvin jettisons Rheya.

Opposite: 'Everything we have done is forgiven.'

choosing projects that ignore that image. His alliance with Soderbergh, both as an actor and co-producer, shows a taste for challenge. Here, as Kelvin, he is intelligent, withdrawn, sad, puzzled.'[94]

Looking back on the film, Soderbergh blames himself for the film's shortcomings: 'I had, to a person, a cast that was very willing and very, very capable. That was a movie that I struggled with. There was some restructuring and reshooting. It's a movie that's frustrating for me to think about, because I think there's good stuff in it and there's stuff that I don't think I figured out – to my satisfaction, certainly. That's frustrating because I look at it and I think I had everything I needed: I had complete freedom, I had a great cast. In retrospect, I think what I should've done was brought in one of my super-smart writer friends to help me solve some of the problems I was trying to solve. For whatever reason, maybe because I felt so inside of it, I didn't do that. My memory of the experience is everybody being there absolutely willing and able to give me whatever I wanted, and my at times struggling with what exactly I did want.'[95] But he is unequivocal on Clooney's portrayal of Kelvin: 'It's a really terrific performance. I think because of the reception of the movie, it doesn't get a lot of attention, but he's great in it.'[96]

To his credit, Clooney continued to promote the film throughout Europe even after it had bombed in the US. Though it was not a Section

Eight production, this was exactly the kind of movie the star wanted to make. It was an insanely risky project that, from the scripting stage, would have been scrapped had one of the most popular actors on the planet not thrown his weight behind it. That it got made on a comfortable budget was probably more a result of Cameron's clout at Fox, but as the face of the movie, Clooney sacrificed as much in leverage as he might have gained in critical esteem. However, a decade removed from the film's release, Cameron was right: this is a significant motion picture.

And Clooney has yet to give a better performance. He convincingly expresses heart-breakingly specific shades of sadness that feel more genuine than anything he had given the audience before. His reaction to jettisoning the first iteration of Rheya into space is so authentic that it feels like a violation to witness it. This is the weird thing about movie stars – when they give themselves up, when they are believably helpless, they can pulverize. It is like James Stewart breaking down at the end of Anthony Mann's *The Naked Spur* (1953): the emotion itself is devastating enough, but the fearlessness of the act somehow elevates it. Of course, as often occurs in Hollywood, Clooney would soon be honoured for a fine performance that is a fraction as impressive as his work in *Solaris*.

6

Bob Barnes

Syriana (2005)
Stephen Gaghan

'Your entire career you've been used, and
probably never even known what for.'
'I didn't used to need to know.'
—Dean Whiting / Bob Barnes

Following the commercial and critical let-down
of *Solaris* and *Confessions of a Dangerous Mind*,
Clooney once again teamed up with Joel and
Ethan Coen in 2003 for *Intolerable Cruelty*,
a licentious farce that comes on like Ernst
Lubitsch's *Trouble in Paradise* (1932) only
to get fall-down drunk on its own misanthropy.
The Coens have always had an ear for classic
screwball comedy cadence, and few actors
alive today possess Clooney's gift for rapid-
fire elocution. But what could have been a late-
breaking, worthy-of-Hawks depiction of a heel's
reformation turns into an uneasy negotiation
between preening cynicism and studio-mandated
sentimentality. It is a shame, because Clooney's
portrayal of Miles Massey, a jackass of a divorce
lawyer (whose success is such that an air-tight
prenuptial agreement bears his name), is the
closest he has come to approximating the gleeful
guile of Cary Grant's Walter Burns from Howard
Hawks' *His Girl Friday* (1940) – with Catherine
Zeta-Jones, as an avaricious divorcee, dexterously
deflecting his verbal onslaught. It is a strange kind
of failure: the elements are in place and often
interact brilliantly, but the Coens never bring
it above simmer.

Despite this string of disappointments, the
idea of George Clooney was as popular as ever
in Hollywood; Section Eight was viewed as
the most exciting production house in town
(a hothouse of unfettered invention and creative
integrity), while his unabashed liberalism – at
a time when 'liberal' was held in roughly the
same regard as 'fascist' in the United States –
earned him a great deal of admiration in the
traditionally left-leaning town. Artists felt
emboldened to attack the post-9/11 paranoia
and fury that had led the country into two
concurrent wars, and, in lieu of any significant
films addressing this issue, they were cheered
that at least one major movie star was using
his clout to make a stand against the
madness. This is the type of thing Hollywood
likes to reward. They were about to get their
chance.

Who's Afraid of 'Harvey Milquetoast'?

In the weeks following the attacks of
11 September 2001, Steven Soderbergh sent his
Traffic screenwriter Stephen Gaghan an early copy
of Robert Baer's memoir, *See No Evil: The True
Story of a Ground Soldier in the CIA's War on
Terrorism*. Baer's book was a fiery indictment of
an agency undone by Beltway bureaucracy and
turf scuffles; it was a chesty airing of grievances
from a former CIA spy who had been cast aside
for what he considered a more politically correct
and less worldly type of agent – and these
institutional shifts were, in his estimation,
reflective of the failings that caused 9/11. But
while Baer was an international man of intrigue,
he was not exactly James Bond. And when
Gaghan set out to write a screenplay suggested
by *See No Evil*, he was not in the market for
a debonair movie star for the Baer-inspired role
of Bob Barnes. 'He's "Harvey Milquetoast"', said
Gaghan, describing the character as a nondescript
everyman.[97] 'And what is a movie star if not the
opposite of Harvey Milquetoast?'[98] But when
Clooney got a hold of the Section Eight-shepherded
script, he knew he wanted in. 'I called up Gaghan
and he said, "I really don't want a movie star in
this role." I agreed: I said I can play this part, but
I'm going to need thirty days to change a little bit.
So I shaved my hairline back about an inch and
a half, grew a beard and put on thirty pounds
in thirty days. And when we told Warners that
we were going to do it for no money, it's hard
to say no to that.'[99] The temptation to transform
one's carefully cultivated image is a common
one for actors; it is a tremendous physical
challenge that allows for a more complete
character immersion (and, if done convincingly,
the admiration of one's peers). But once one
passes forty years old, packing on excess pounds
can be a rigorous experience.

It is also hard to gain weight when one has
maintained a trim-ish figure most of one's adult
life. 'The truth is it's not nearly as fun as it sounds,
the idea of putting on that kind of weight,' recalls
Clooney, 'but at the end of the day, in general,
that's what we do for a living. So my job was just
to eat as fast as I could, as much as I could… But
you just ate until you wanted to throw up, and
made sure you didn't throw up. So that was my

Clooney gained weight to play
Bob Barnes, a diminished CIA
field agent, in *Syriana* (2005),
directed by Stephen Gaghan.

Following pages: Barnes flees
an anti-tank missile explosion.

job for a month, was eating.'[100] To complete the transformation, Clooney summoned Baer to his Lake Como estate in Italy for a week of acclimatization to the unglamorous spy lifestyle. Never one for a method-actor approach, Clooney mostly probed Baer for insights into his disillusionment with the agency. His intellectual curiosity would help him understand the shadowy world Baer once inhabited, which, on camera, was manifested physically as a jittery paranoia.

Oil-Slick Morality

Had *Syriana* been left to the heavy hands of an Oliver Stone or Paul Haggis, Gaghan's sprawling dramatization of petro-politics and Middle East arms trafficking might have been simplified to reflect a white-hat/black-hat conflict between the corrupt and the true believers. But Gaghan's script is a daring blur of shifting morality; save for a few bad actors, everyone is pursuing their own interest for what they believe are the right reasons. Barnes is scrambling to stop the politically suspect assassination of the progressive young Prince Nasir (Alexander Siddig); energy analyst Bryan Woodman (Matt Damon) is attempting to maintain his objectivity while being wined and dined by the family of an unnamed oil-rich country; DC lawyer Bennett Holiday (Jeffrey Wright) is promoting the 'illusion of due diligence' in an oil company merger while contending with an alcoholic father; and the impressionable Pakistani migrant worker Wasim Khan (Mazhar Munir) falls under the spell of a radical Islamist cleric who sells martyrdom as a viable option to a lifetime of unceasing poverty. 'Obviously, *Syriana* was sort of a head-on hunt', Clooney told *The Hollywood Reporter* in 2006, 'But I thought it was such a well-crafted script that that was fair enough to do. You have to be careful how you do those, remembering that there's a way that you end up hurting the cause that you're trying to help. It's a very tricky balance, but I do enjoy watching social and political comment in film again. I've missed it for twenty years.'[101] Clooney had signed on to the film before the myriad Democrat defeats of the 2004 elections, but it clearly communicates a nuanced frustration with the state of the world, and, most provocatively, the oil-mad machinations that impoverished a region (save for the royals) and gave rise to a deadly religious fanaticism. There are epigrammatic exchanges designed to provoke mild fist-pumps (particularly in Barnes's sit-down with a puppet master law firm exec, Dean Whiting, played with moneyed arrogance by Christopher Plummer), but Gaghan assiduously avoids pat resolutions. No one is saving the world in these 128 minutes, but the viewer might emerge from the theatre with a finer appreciation for The Way Things Are. And Clooney's Barnes is the ultimate mid-level employee with whom audiences can identify:

a paunchy, bearded, put-upon lifer who knows his job, much to the chagrin of the corrupt upper-management. Clooney has never looked more like a regular guy in his entire career, and he is unlikely to put himself through that heavyset hell again.

The Accident

Whether Clooney was absent of worldly concerns prior to the moment he flopped over in a chair and cracked his head on the floor is open to speculation (he is not saying); what is certain is that he has subsequently lived every day with headaches ranging from tolerable to awful. The mishap in question occurred during *Syriana*'s brutal torture scene in which Barnes has his fingernails torn out by a mercenary (Mark Strong) he previously hired to kill Prince Nasir. The inquisitor wants Barnes to give up names of people who have taken money from the US government; the more Barnes resists, the more fingernails he will extract via pliers. It is a striking scene: Strong proves a frighteningly comfortable inquisitor, while the viewer is acutely aware that Barnes will not relinquish his honour willingly; this is going to be a brutally protracted process, and there is no reason to believe Gaghan will skimp on the gory details. But on a superficial level one cannot help but note Clooney's state of physical dishevelment. This is a man who has let himself go, who has eaten well and worked out infrequently. He has not given up yet; he is still fighting the good fight and trying to halt an unjust air strike. But he is aware of his encroaching irrelevance and, therefore, his own mortality. This is clear before he is tortured, which makes his fingernail-shedding defiance all the more poignant. His loyalty is unappreciated, yet here he is taking an overwhelming beating for principles that have long been eschewed by his employer. Barnes's reward? He dies unceremoniously, trying to do the right thing. It is an inconvenient sacrifice that will be celebrated by no one.

The torture scene is twice as harrowing once one takes into consideration the life-altering injury Clooney sustained during its filming. 'It was my own dumb fault', he joked at a press conference. 'I was taped to a chair and a guy was pretending to hit me. It's all fake, you're not really getting punched, and I flipped myself over on the chair, and cracked my head and tore what's called my dura, which is the wrapping around your spine, and ended up with what they call a CSF leak, which is a cranial spinal fluid leak – good fun. I highly recommend it for everybody out there.'[102] This was his response in 2005; it was not until 2012 that he finally acknowledged the full severity of the accident.

A Kodak Misstep

Syriana may be the 'jewel in the crown' of Section Eight's existence: it is an intentionally obfuscated

The torture scene, which ended up with Clooney's accident.

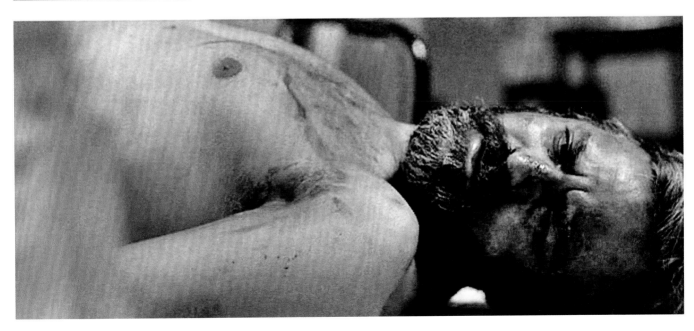

account of petro-politics that works best as a deep-tissue character study of four very different men (Barnes, Woodman, Holiday and Khan). There is no chance a film this rigorously intellectual would have been given the green light without the backing of two major movie stars – especially with a largely unproven director at the helm (Gaghan's first movie, *Abandon*, 2002, was a low-aiming misfire). The immediate critical response to *Syriana* was mostly positive, with a preponderance of raves offsetting a smattering of baffled pans (the majority of which amounted to surrender in the face of too much minutiae). Little has changed on the geopolitical stage since *Syriana*'s theatrical release, but the film does play nowadays like a time capsule of outrage gone by; Bush's executive office misbehaviour has been replaced by Obama's indifference to drone strikes and unlawful surveillance. It is also a film that is far more damning in the explaining than in execution; visually, it feels like Gaghan is grasping for B-roll – a collage of humdrum Middle Eastern living – to maintain the viewer's interest while he unloads a tanker full of exposition pertaining to the murderously corrupt oil industry.

But Clooney is right there at the centre of the film doing what a movie star is supposed to do. Though he is buried under a beard and thirty extra pounds, he puts a human face to an almost incomprehensible tangle of double-dealing and state-sponsored murder. He is the guy who paints

the target, but he wants to know that the target deserves the payload. Clooney often appears suffocated by the physical weight; more intriguingly, Barnes must deal with his pissed-off son from a failed marriage. There is a crushing burden of professional and family obligations from which Barnes cannot extricate himself; Clooney has played a father before, but this is the first time it tracks as something real. And yet it is quite clear Clooney is on vacation from the bachelor lifestyle; by the time he was campaigning for a Best Supporting Actor Oscar, he had shed the flab and shaved the beard.

There is an entire industry dedicated to Hollywood's award season and it is rarely governed by a genuine reaction to a film's quality, but when a movie star undergoes a physical transformation (and nearly dies in the process), voters will swoon. Bob Barnes is not close to Clooney's best performance; every chapter previous to this, save for *Ocean's Eleven*, is evidence of greater ingenuity. But 2005 was deemed his year and so he found his way to the Dolby Theatre (formerly the Kodak Theatre) stage to collect his first Academy Award – which occasioned the first significant public misstep of his career. For a man who has skilfully avoided the pitfalls of entertainment industry smugness, he delivered a catastrophically self-congratulatory acceptance speech, including the following self-righteous reflection: '... we are a little bit

Above: Bob Barnes with Bryan Woodman (Matt Damon), Prince Nasir Al-Subaai (Alexander Siddig).

Opposite: A bearded, bulkier Clooney.

Following pages: Screenwriter and director, Stephen Gaghan, with George Clooney on the set of the film.

out of touch in Hollywood every once in a while, I think. It's probably a good thing. We're the ones who talked about AIDS when it was just being whispered, and we talked about civil rights when it wasn't really popular. And we, you know, we bring up subjects, we are the ones – this Academy, this group of people gave Hattie McDaniel an Oscar in 1940 when blacks were still sitting in the backs of theaters. I'm proud to be a part of this Academy, proud to be part of this community, and proud to be out of touch. And I thank you so much for this.'

This is, like the films *Syriana* so defiantly avoids, a tone-deaf message to the converted – most of whom are white. It is not, in the least, an insincere oration; Clooney's embrace of Hollywood's progressiveness was likely an angry reaction to his father getting repeatedly criticized in the State of his birth for having the temerity to raise a son who is handsome, successful and opinionated. Clooney had the right to fire back, but he did so in an entitled fashion, leaving himself open to justified criticism from Spike Lee: 'To use that as an example of how progressive Hollywood is is ridiculous. Hattie McDaniel played Mammy in *Gone with the Wind*. That film was basically saying that the wrong side won the Civil War and that black people should still be enslaved. C'mon! I like George a lot. I'm not hating on him. But I don't think he really thought it out.'[103] But the most stinging retort to Clooney's speech

came from his buddies at *South Park*, who built their 29 March 2006 episode 'Smug Alert!' around a deadly 'smug cloud' emanating from the actor's Academy Awards speech. The cloud creates a 'perfect storm of self-satisfaction' that ravages South Park, where citizens have become overly enamoured and boastful of their hybrid automobiles. It is a sharp jab at modern liberalism, and it draws a little blood because the bad guy in this scenario is the man who made the show possible. Clooney was riding a little too high, which is a good time to humble oneself. He had fortunately one of the meatiest roles of his career waiting for him.

Above: Barnes serving as the CIA's unwitting pawn.

Opposite: On 30 April 2006, in Washington, DC, thousands of people rallied on the National Mall at the United States Capitol to end the genocide in Darfur. Actor George Clooney led the cause after just finishing a trip to the region.

Following pages: Barnes and Mussawi (Mark Strong) talk dirty business.

Once George Clooney became a fixture in the global superstar firmament, he was presented with the perilous opportunity to use his popularity to drive attention and money toward a cause near and dear to his heart. Movie stars and rock singers are often ridiculed for supporting causes about which they know little – and in some cases it is true that one's desire to, say, protect the Amazonian rain forest is as much about burnishing a legacy as actually making a difference in the world. Being both savvy and allergic to hypocrisy, Clooney knew that when he went to the mat for the powerless victims of genocide in Darfur and South Sudan, he would have to become an expert on the subject. 'Whatever your [political] inclination is, first and foremost, if you're going to jump into it, you gotta be ready to take a hit – because that's going to happen. And you have to be incredibly well-informed. So if you're going to go and talk about poverty or AIDS in Africa or Darfur, you better know your shit. And you better know it better than any of the jackasses that are going to try and somehow make what you're trying to do [look] bad. There's another problem when you try and do too many of these causes. Things start to get… muddled, right. So you have to pick your fights and go after them, and then it seems like you can help get things done.'[10] Clooney's interest in the Darfur conflict was aroused in 2006, when he participated in a 'Save Darfur' rally in Washington, DC; he later participated in the Don Cheadle-produced activist documentary *Darfur Now* (2007). In 2007, along with Cheadle, Matt Damon, Brad Pitt, David Pressman and Jerry Weintraub, Clooney launched the Not On Our Watch project, which subsequently initiated the Satellite Sentinel Project, designed to monitor, predict and prevent the carrying out of mass atrocities by Sudanese warlords. In also serving as a UN Messenger of Peace from 2008 to 2014, Clooney has gone well beyond donning a T-shirt and cutting a few commercials. He has brought attention to an easily ignored humanitarian crisis and, just maybe, saved a few lives.

7

Michael Clayton

Michael Clayton (2007)
Tony Gilroy

'I'm not the guy you kill. I'm the guy you buy!'
—Michael Clayton

Clooney's triumphant 2005 gave way to an unintentionally quiet 2006 – the hush being provided by the critical and commercial indifference to the Soderbergh-directed *The Good German*. Based on Joseph Kanon's morally ambiguous novel, the film stars Clooney as American journalist Jake Geismer, a cynical sort who has dropped in on post-war Germany in 1945 to reconnect with his former flame, Lena Brandt (Cate Blanchett), who is now married to a coveted German rocket scientist. The film is a thematically ambitious attempt to deglamorize the classic American war movie as found within the aesthetic trappings of beloved works such as *Casablanca* (1942). But Soderbergh does not stage the picture with the black and white, expressionistic flair of a Michael Curtiz; instead, he feels hemmed in by the careful framing and pace, which renders the film strangely discordant and inert. This is especially disappointing because Clooney and Blanchett often go at their roles with a dramatically heightened vigour; they are game for melodrama but Soderbergh seems apprehensive about following them there.

Post-Oscar Anxiety

Clooney's distaste for typical leading man roles in banal studio movies left him with a paucity of options as he scanned the post-Oscar landscape for work. Edging ever closer to fifty, and getting an inkling of his own mortality (a notion surely reinforced by the unremitting discomfort from his accident on the set of *Syriana*), Clooney was eager to get back in front of the camera, but the scripts simply were not there – or so he thought. In actual fact, he had already read and turned down the screenplay that would earn him his first Academy Award nomination for Best Performance by an Actor in a Leading Role. 'Steven [Soderbergh] called me up and said you should do [*Michael Clayton*]', remembers Clooney. 'I read it, and I thought yes, it's a really good script, but I was in the middle of doing *Good Night, and Good Luck* [released in 2005] so I wasn't anxious to jump and do anything

else. I'm very careful to work with first-time directors. I had worries. I thought this is a really tricky piece of material, really well written, but there's a lot of traps. It could end up being jokey, which it can't be, if you're not incredibly adept.'[104]

The first-time director was Tony Gilroy, who had also written the actor's feast of a screenplay about a corporate law firm fixer who inadvisably grows a conscience after one of his colleagues turns up dead. Understanding Clooney's reticence, but also knowing the script was an absolute knockout, Soderbergh kept pressing his friend. 'A couple of years go by', says Soderbergh, 'and he's finished *Syriana*. We're talking on the phone, and he said, "I can't find anything. I want to go to work, and I can't find anything." I said, "Do yourself a favor: go back and read *Michael Clayton*." He did, and he said, "Wow, it's better than I remember." I said, "Just get in a room with Tony."'[105]

'We finally met after I finished *Good Night, and Good Luck*', said Clooney. 'I spent a seven or eight hour lunch with Tony, who I had never met before. We hung out. By the end of it, on top of thinking he could handle it, you just liked him. Somehow that makes a big difference in filmmaking. You go, I think that this guy knows what he wants and I believe he knows how to get it.'[106] Meanwhile, Gilroy, a veteran of the studio screenwriter trenches who was ready to cash in on the clout he had acquired via writing *The Bourne Identity* and its two blockbuster sequels, was savvy enough to understand Clooney's value to the production. 'George is such a quietly ambitious actor', Gilroy said. 'Look at the roles he's choosing and the things he's doing along the way. He was the grand prize in this whole thing. There was no way of making this movie without him working for free. He becomes this security blanket, the ultimate protection who makes sure nobody messes with the movie.'[107]

Had this been the 1970s or the early 1980s, Clooney probably would not have had to take such a drastic pay cut to get the movie a green light. The film would be the penultimate Section Eight release,[108] with distribution via Clooney's long-time home studio of Warner Bros. For Clooney, the appeal of playing Clayton was

Tony Gilroy chose Clooney for the part of Michael Clayton, a facilitator in a law firm, in *Michael Clayton* (2007).

109

Opposite: Called upon in the middle of the night to fix a 'situation', Clayton drives to a wealthy client's home.

Following pages: Arthur Edens (Tom Wilkinson) is released into Clayton's custody after melting down during a deposition.

obvious: it was reminiscent of arguably his favourite movie star's finest performance. 'There isn't any actor who doesn't like a role in this', he said. 'These are the characters that, if you caught the movie 10 years earlier in their life, they're the bad guy. Like Paul Newman in *The Verdict* – I'm certainly not comparing my acting, just talking about those kinds of characters – or Clint Eastwood in *Unforgiven*. Those characters did a lot of terrible things and now they're searching for some sort of redemption.'[109] Newman was fifty-seven in *The Verdict*, and playing a lawyer much further down on the judicial food chain, but Clayton offered Clooney the opportunity to play a past-his-prime attorney charged with doing behind-the-scenes dirty work for his firm's wealthy clients. As Gilroy described it, 'Kicking mistresses out of apartments, killing stories with journalists, getting somebody's wife out of a shoplifting charge, I don't think anybody knows what that takes out of someone like Clayton. Least of all the people who pay them to do it. I'd been trying to develop that character for a while. There's nothing sadder than being too late in one's career and life, like Clayton. You go back to *The Verdict* or *Save the Tiger* or *The Entertainer* – the idea of someone who had a chance to do something and blew it, is very appealing material for writers and actors.'[110] For Clooney, this meant exploring for the first time a life on the verge of being wasted – something that surely struck a resonant chord given his Great Uncle George Guilfoyle's final words. Clayton is a man who is just old and irrelevant enough to see the unremarkable epitaph being inscribed on his tombstone – and while he is angry and bitter about it, he is powerless to do anything about it.

The Fixer's Lament

When the viewer first sees Michael Clayton, he is frittering away some time at an underground poker game in New York City. Before heading home for the night, he is called upon to 'fix' a hit-and-run accident for one of the firm's well-off clients. This is usually the scene where the protagonist displays his expertise – which, in this case, would be performing some kind of mop-up miracle like Harvey Keitel's Winston Wolfe in *Pulp Fiction*. Clayton's boss, Walter (Thomas McCarthy), might have promised his client a 'miracle worker', but what he has got in Clayton is a pragmatist. 'There's no play here', explains Clayton. 'There's no angle. There's no champagne room. I'm not a miracle worker. I'm a janitor. The math on this is simple: the smaller the mess, the easier it is for me to clean up.' Clayton rattles this off with an air of detachment that verges on contempt; it is not a matter of if the wealthy client will accept

his solution, but when. Still, the client gesticulates and rants, filling his tastefully furnished kitchen with privileged indignation while Clayton remains calm. Clayton finally leaves the client's impressive country estate and drives off into the early morning light. Along the way, he stops his car and inexplicably walks out into a field to a small group of horses; while reaching out to them, his car explodes in the distance.

Gilroy hurtles the narrative backwards four days, and skilfully builds back to this moment over a brisk 100 minutes. Along the way, he sandwiches Clooney between two overpoweringly showy performances from Tilda Swinton (as agribusiness general counsel Karen Crowder) and Tom Wilkinson (the manic-depressive Arthur Edens, whose wayward defence of said agribusiness thrusts him into a bizarre romance with a young plaintiff named Anna [Merritt Wever]). In *The Verdict* and *Save the Tiger* (1973), the movie star *was* the show; in *Michael Clayton*, Clooney is stuck giving one of his finest, most nuanced performances in the middle of a thespian fireworks display. Clayton's assignment is to bail Edens out of jail (for contemptuously shedding his clothes during a deposition while hysterically professing his love to Anna), get him back on his medication and, no matter how unlikely, back into the courtroom. But Edens is too far gone, and U-North, the agricultural giant whose class action suit he has decided to undermine, wants him out of the picture permanently. Clayton is already beginning to take seriously Edens's claims of intentional wrongdoing by U-North before his friend is murdered; when he realizes the sheer scope of the company's duplicity (including Crowder's order to have Edens and, ultimately, Clayton rubbed out), he stealthily elicits a confession from Crowder while wearing a wire for the Feds.

Playing Facilitator

What is a guy to do when he finds himself in an actor's showcase where the two meatiest roles belong to supporting players? It is a thankless task, but he has got to be the (relatively) quiet, sturdy star around which his fellow performers orbit before burning themselves out in a hail of histrionics. In other words, along with not drawing a salary for his acting services in *Michael Clayton*, Clooney was also playing set-up man to two of the best actors in the business. For the basketball-loving Clooney, this is akin to playing point guard in a five-on-five game; his job is to set up the two most talented scorers on the court, and let them reap the glory. Considering that Wilkinson earned a Best Supporting Actor nomination and Swinton a Best Supporting Actress win, he fulfilled his role brilliantly.

Opposite, top: Clayton tries
desperately to pull Edens
back from the precipice
of madness.

Opposite, bottom: Clayton
on the phone, attempting
to fix his personal life.

On his way back from
Westchester, Clayton stops
his car to see about horses.
While reaching out to them,
his car explodes in the distance.

Following pages: Clayton
makes a last-ditch effort
to save Edens.

And yet on repeated viewings, it is Clooney's portrayal of a man trying to do one selfless thing after a lifetime of covering tracks for the selfish that is most rewarding. He is a failure who found a disreputable niche, and he has been thriving within that niche for so long that he has lost sight of anything resembling a purpose. His marriage fell apart, the restaurant he started with his drug-addict brother collapsed in a heap of debt and he is a barely functional father to his young son. Clooney might have won an Oscar for playing a discarded professional in *Syriana* but one feels the weight of disappointment and regret far more palpably here; the lack of a physical transformation – and, of course, the additional screen time, given that he is the protagonist of the film – allows Clooney to paint a more accurate (i.e. closer-to-the-bone) portrait of resignation. There is also a poignant mentor–protégé dynamic between Clooney and Pollack, who, in his penultimate performance, evinces a subtle wistfulness in his scenes with a star he probably would have given anything to direct. Clooney does get a chance to come out swinging at the end when Clayton gives Crowder her comeuppance (delivering the delicious kiss-off, 'I am Shiva, the God of Death'), but, in keeping with the rest of the film, he gets his best moment over the closing credits. After turning Crowder over to the authorities (who, given the abundance of evidence he has given them via

wire, will no doubt prosecute her to the fullest), Clooney walks out of a hotel and hails a cab. 'Give me fifty dollars worth', he instructs the cabbie. 'Just drive.' And very slowly a sense of relief washes over that classic visage; his muscles untighten and the early stages of a grin break out. Clayton is at last unburdened: he cannot undo the wreckage of the past, but he can look his son in the face with a clear conscience. It is a crowd-pleasing denouement (the optimistic flipside of the 1970s paranoid thrillers that inspired it), but it feels earned. The scene is even more impressive when you realize it was shot on the streets of Manhattan during the day, and that regular New Yorkers were calling out his name as the car inched its way through traffic. Taking this into consideration, one can see the character of Clayton merge with Clooney the public figure: the former enjoying his newfound spiritual peace, while the latter soaks in an unexpected curtain call.

In Clooney's estimation, it is not salvation but rather a backing away from spiritual oblivion. 'The way it reads, it doesn't feel very redemptive. It's not a big gotcha kind of film. Arthur dies. I don't get a job. If you made *It's a Wonderful Life* [1946] today, they'd have to haul Lionel Barrymore off at the end and put him in jail. That's how the bad guy has to get got. The reason that movie's a perfect film is because the redemption comes through the fact that

Jimmy Stewart gets to go home to his family and say, hey, you know what, living well is the greatest revenge. In this film, everybody doesn't have to get got. You're buying tiny bits, increments of what makes us all human. People become the bad guys rather gradually. I don't think they start off saying, "Oh, I know what I'll do." You do incrementally stupid things that you figure, well, this helps my family, I can justify it. And you wake up one day and it's Tyco.'[111]

October Surprise

There were many other thoroughbreds running in the 2007 fall awards derby, but *Michael Clayton*, with its first-time filmmaker and unassuming title, broke out immediately with a flourish of ecstatic reviews. The *Boston Globe*'s Ty Burr raved, 'Clooney, for his part, allows his movie star looks to go flabby and soft (all things being relative, of course), and he buries the performance way down in his gut.'[112] Roger Ebert disagreed with Burr's assessment of Clooney's physical fitness, but he was equally as enthusiastic: 'Clooney looks as if he stepped into the role from the cover of *GQ*. It's the right look. Conservative suit, tasteful tie, clean shaven, every hair in place (except when things are going wrong, which is often).'[113] (Regarding Clayton's extra weight, Clooney told *The New Yorker*, 'I didn't want him to be in really rocking shape.'[114])

There was, however, one curiously harsh takedown offered up by *The Guardian*'s Josh Spero. 'George Clooney's range of expressions is limited thus: 1) suave amusement; 2) suave distress; 3) suave amusement. Watching him try to pull his features into a rictus of despair in *Michael Clayton* this weekend I realised that there's no shame in sticking within your range. This is why typecasting is such a success.'[115] This hit piece, titled 'George Clooney should stick to being suave', might be the harshest bit of acting criticism ever written about Clooney, though it undercuts its effectiveness (even if intended as a jest), by offering up this contradictory, and lazily catty, observation: 'When he tries to do suave, though – well, he makes Cary Grant look like Vincent Price.'[116]

For Soderbergh, who played a pivotal role in attaching Clooney to *Michael Clayton*, the performance ranks as one of his very best: 'I was happy to be a part of getting him in that movie, because I think it's a great movie and he's great in it. That was one of those things where… on the one hand, you see people give performances that are very good performances, but there are external things… there are fewer people who can do what George does in that movie. What he does in that movie not a lot of people can do. The way he centers that film, the way he shoulders it, that's harder than a lot of things that pass for amazing acting.'[117]

If George Clooney's directing career fails to follow the triumphant upward trajectory of his acting oeuvre, perhaps it is because he saves his greatest risks for the films that belong exclusively to him. As he has shown throughout his career, he can withstand critical and commercial failure provided the rejection is honest; for the most part, Clooney would be the first to own up to the shortcomings of his directorial efforts. Clooney was still finding his way as a filmmaker when he took a crack at Chuck Barris's embellished autobiography *Confessions of a Dangerous Mind*, in which the creator of *The Dating Game* and *The Gong Show* portrayed himself as a part-time assassin for the CIA. The screenplay by Charlie Kaufman was considered one of Hollywood's best unproduced scripts – an assessment Clooney shared, but this did not stop him from toning down the more out-there notions of the *Being John Malkovich* screenwriter. This upset Kaufman, but it is pretty clear that Clooney viewed the film as an experimental playground in which he could try out weird aesthetics to see if they might fit his sensibilities. Clooney and *Three Kings* cinematographer Newton Thomas Sigel mixed up different kinds of film stock, including a weird infrared look for flashback scenes; Clooney also called upon unconventional leading man Sam Rockwell to play the off-kilter Barris, with Drew Barrymore co-starring as his equally idiosyncratic girlfriend. At a 2002 press conference for the film, Clooney remarked, 'You might as well work with the best. I have the best cinematographer, I have the best editor, I have the best sound guy. I got all the people, I called in all my favors to work with people that I thought, "Why not work with the best people I can?"'[p] Working with these skilled professionals undoubtedly helped Clooney learn on the fly, but the movie never feels like more than a lark; it is a two-hour film-school assignment undone by muddled visuals and clashing tones. But it is a fascinating failure that only a talented director could make. As a first-time director, Barrymore had only praise for Clooney: 'He gives you incredible suggestions that you weren't thinking to go there. Most of those takes are what's in the movie. [He has] just a really amazing way of articulating what his vision is and what he wants. He's very loving and very nurturing, but he's just incredibly objective.'[q] Select any random magazine profile of Clooney, and he will invariably tell the interviewer, proudly, that he is the 'son of

a newsman'. Nick Clooney had immense respect for the great broadcasters of his day, particularly Edward R. Murrow, so it was only natural that his son would go on to lionize the legendary reporter in film form. But the result, *Good Night, and Good Luck* (2005), is not a standard-issue biopic; it is an ensemble entertainment built around Murrow's on-air investigation into US Senator Joseph McCarthy's overreaching crusade to expunge all traces of communism from the government. As director and co-writer (with Grant Heslov), Clooney takes the supporting role of *See It Now* producer Fred Friendly, who backs up the bold Murrow (David Strathairn) as he risks his professional career to call out a bully who is recklessly destroying innocent civilians' lives. The film is presented in black and white for a couple of reasons: 1) Clooney has a deep nostalgia for that period of broadcasting (as revealed by his live broadcasts) and 2) he wanted McCarthy to play himself. 'I knew right off the bat that we wanted the old footage of McCarthy because I thought no actor could play him. No one would believe that anyone in that situation could be that much of a buffoon. No one could giggle like a hyena and be believable. So we wanted to use the real footage in the same way Murrow used the footage of McCarthy to hang him.'[r] This left Strathairn the formidable challenge of not only capturing Murrow's stentorian authority, but also of seeming as much a part of the era as McCarthy. He credits both the on and off-screen Clooney for helping him to pull off the illusion: '[Clooney has] not only a technical understanding, but a feel for the time – and then as an actor, a generosity of

spirit, knowing what actors need to do their best work, what kind of direction, or how much or how little, and also how to provide a safety net for them out there. He was on top of it, really. He absolutely knows what he's doing."[s] Upon seeing the film, Steven Soderbergh warned Clooney he might have done too good a job: 'I remember sitting at the bar of the Cipriani in Venice after the screening and saying, "I think you've made a perfect movie. You need to be prepared for the fact that it may be a long time before you make something like that again. That doesn't mean you won't make something good. I'm just saying I think that's a perfect film." It's just great. Everything's right. Those are rare.'[t] Soderbergh's prophecy proved accurate. With the exception of the intriguingly cynical *The Ides of March* (2011), Clooney's directorial efforts have fallen far short of *Good Night, and Good Luck*. *Leatherheads* (2008), a 1920s-set comedy about a foundering professional football league, is a sporadically funny sports film that becomes lumpy

and unfocused when it takes on the endangered sanctity of American journalism (exemplified by the revelation of a star player's bogus war heroics). Clooney insisted the film was 'not designed to change the world – it's just designed to be good fun'.[u] Had he stuck to that edict, he would have had a smashing screwball comedy. Six years later, Clooney stumbled badly with *The Monuments Men* (2014), a men-on-a-mission World War II film in which the soldiers' expertise is art history not fighting. Clooney leads an all-star group of actors behind enemy lines to recover some of the most important works of art in human history. It is a fabulous idea for a movie, but is it meant to be a jaunty tribute to these unlikely soldiers, or a sombre meditation on the civilizing power of great art? Clooney cannot get a grasp on the tone, and, as a result, it stands as his biggest artistic failure to date. However, in the meantime, Clooney had made *The Ides of March*, where his direction is shown to be fluid and restrained. 'He's sort of possessed by the film while

he's making it', said his co-star Ryan Gosling.[v] It is evident that he wanted to deliver a film for adults that is as entertaining as it is intellectually satisfying. 'I've been doing this for a long time, and all I really want to do is make films that I'm proud of later in life. This is one of those.'[w] Perhaps the most interesting observation from Clooney came while the actor was doing press in London in January 2012: 'I've had some success at writing and directing, and I like it. It's infinitely more creative than just acting and I have things I want to say and do. I feel like I've been given these keys and the ability to drive the old man's car, and I know they're going to take the keys away at some point, so I want to drive it as much as I possibly can.'[x]

Page 121: Clooney
with Patricia Clarkson and
Robert Downey, Jr during
the shooting of *Good Night,
and Good Luck* (2005).

Opposite: Clayton
outmanoeuvres U-North
legal counsel Karen
Crowder (Tilda Swinton).

Above: In a cab, Clayton
gets his fifty-dollars worth.

Michael Clayton performed reasonably well at the US box office with a final gross of $49 million, but it did not make much of an impression elsewhere (where it took in only $43 million). There was, however, no need to panic, as *Ocean's Thirteen* (2007) had once again bolstered Clooney's commercial reputation with solid, if unspectacular, grosses in all corners of the globe.

8

Ryan Bingham

Up in the Air (2009)
Jason Reitman

'Life's better with company.'
—Ryan Bingham

As had become customary for Clooney at this point in his career, 2008 qualified as an 'off' year compared to the very 'on' year of 2007. The delayed release of *Leatherheads* forced the actor to do a vigorous round of publicity in support of the movie, but the two most important events for Clooney in 2008 were off screen: the presidential campaign for Barack Obama (to which he contributed in myriad ways) and the establishment of the Not On Our Watch project, which sought to monitor and halt human rights violations in western Sudan (a.k.a. Darfur) while providing aid to the citizens of the war-torn African region.

The Moment

There are three prominent late-summer movie festivals that signal the beginning of what has become known as the 'awards season': the brief, weekend-long Telluride Film Festival, the August Venice Film Festival and the two-week pandemonium of the Toronto International Film Festival. It is hardest to make one's mark in Toronto, which is choked with a large competition slate, star-studded special premieres and twice as many parties. Many distributors and publicists hedge their bets by opening a week earlier at Venice if they are unsure of their product, as a failure to launch at Toronto is catastrophic to a film's awards chances. It is almost impossible to decisively win the buzz war at Toronto – but that's exactly what Clooney did in 2009 when he showed up with *The Men Who Stare at Goats*, *The Informant!* (as executive producer) and, most notably, *Up in the Air*.

As HitFix's Drew McWeeny observed at Toronto that year, 'When a star… and not just an indie actor or a recognizable face, but a full-blown no-contest Movie Star… shows up at any festival, they throw the gravity all out of whack.'[118] While Clooney was no stranger to the festival circuit, there was an overwhelming sense that particular year that this was it. He had the full complement of his arsenal: an off-kilter political satire, the farewell offering from Section Eight and a star vehicle meticulously designed to play off of and comment on his perpetual bachelorhood (which, as he turned forty-eight, was entering Warren Beatty 'will he ever' territory). It did not much matter that two of these films – *The Men Who Stare at Goats* and *The Informant!* – basically stiffed as awards contenders; *Up in the Air* was generating raves across the board, suggesting that another Academy Award nomination for Best Actor was sewn up nearly four months in advance of their announcement. And then there was writer–director Jason Reitman coming on strong with self-made comparisons to a Beatty portrait of an aimless and disillusioned Lothario: 'I think *Up in the Air* is me desperately trying to make my *Shampoo* [1975]', said Reitman.[119] '*Shampoo* is oddly a big influence on this; about a guy who lives freely and is not tied down whatsoever; *Shampoo* ends with Warren Beatty on Mulholland [Drive in Los Angeles], looking out over the city, kind of lost, trying to figure out what his next move will be. And that's how I wanted to end this film.'[120] Reitman was calling his shot, and Clooney was backing his move by dominating the one film festival people just do not dominate. By the time the film was released to theatres in December 2009, they were primed to see a movie star bare his soul in a way few had ever dared to do. It felt momentous, and it was – but not for the reasons the filmmaker and his star had intended.

Familiar Scenery

'It's an interesting thing to watch yourself grow older on screen', Clooney told *The Telegraph*'s John Hiscock in 2009. 'I was watching *Up in the Air* and I thought, "Jesus, who's the old gray-haired guy?" And it was me. I never wear make-up for movies and now it's starting to show.'[121]

Clooney's portrayal of Ryan Bingham in *Up in the Air* lands somewhere between Matt King, the panicked soon-to-be-widower in *The Descendants* and *Solaris*'s Chris Kelvin: he has not yet quite fallen apart like the former, and he has not experienced true, life-shattering grief like the latter. Ryan is a man who likes his itinerant life; he genuinely enjoys racking up airline miles as he flies from city to city to personally inform people he has never met that they are out of a job. He is proud of his ability to navigate airport security with ninja-like precision,

Clooney plays Ryan Bingham, a corporate downsizing expert, in the film *Up in the Air* (2009), directed by Jason Reitman.

he satiates his desire for companionship with hotel bar pickups and he is never more miserable than when he is forced to stay in his unadorned Omaha, Nebraska, apartment for more than a few days. Ryan is single. He has no children, but he does have two sisters, and he is begrudgingly pledged to take pictures of a cardboard cut-out of the youngest, Julie (Melanie Lynskey), and her fiancé, Jim (Danny McBride), in front of landmarks in the various cities he visits. What matters most to Ryan, however, is the fact that he is nearing ten million frequent flyer miles: a rare accomplishment that only six travellers have managed to pull off. So when Ryan's boss informs him that the company is looking to cut costs by terminating people via videoconferencing, he is as annoyed by the impersonal nature of the approach as he is by the realization that his frequent-flyer-miles record might be in jeopardy.

Ryan's irritation is compounded by his company's request that he break in a young employee, Natalie Keener (Anna Kendrick). Gone, at least temporarily, are the days of solo travels and occasional, no-fuss hook-ups with his best-friend-with-benefits Alex Goran (Vera Farmiga); he is now charged with teaching this upstart proponent of videoconferencing lay-offs how to do the job he has mastered – only so she can ply her trade on the other end of a laptop from several thousand miles away. But Ryan is a good company man: he takes Natalie on, gives the videoconferencing a disastrous go (turns out the personal touch makes a difference) and even counsels her through an unexpected break-up with her boyfriend. Meanwhile he is able to work in some quality screw time with Alex, to whom he finds himself growing attached. And this is where the cracks in Ryan's facade begin to form: after inviting Alex to his sister's wedding, he begins to yearn for permanence. This ends disastrously when he decides to surprise Alex at her home in Chicago, only to find that she is a happily married mother. Alex later informs Ryan, quite brutally, that he is 'a parenthesis' – i.e. a temporary escape from the mundanity of her normal life. Suddenly, Ryan (and Clooney, who has never more comfortably inhabited a role before or since) is forced to confront the emptiness of his life. He carries almost nothing around, he leaves almost nothing behind and the only people who remember him are the ones whose lives he irrevocably altered, mostly for the worse – though he likes to think his well-rehearsed bullshit sends these people out the door on a triumphal note. 'Anybody who ever built an empire, or changed the world, sat where you are now. And it's *because* they sat there that they were able to do it.'

What's in your Backpack?

Clooney has his movie-star wattage dialled up to blinding as Ryan Bingham, but the idea that this performance or film lands anywhere in the same ballpark as Hal Ashby's *Shampoo* is absurd. It is a comparison that sounds great but fails to take into account one crucial thing: Beatty and Clooney are completely different types of men. The fun, yet ultimately disconcerting, experience of *Shampoo* is watching a shallow swimming pool of a hairdresser work his shambolic charms on women who are as much of a mess as he is. *Up in the Air* spends most of its first act letting us get drunk on the Clooney cocktail. Ryan's airport bar meet-cute with Alex is sharply written; it is Reitman indulging his Billy Wilder side, and standing back as Clooney and Farmiga throw off sparks (who knew comparing corporate benefit cards could be so sexy). These are two adults who know exactly what they are doing and precisely what they want from each other. So while it is true that both films function as snapshots of the times in which they were made, there is a tidiness to Ryan's journey that leaves it feeling mapped out rather than stumbled through. The control works for Clooney: he is in such thorough command of his instrument and his image that he will breeze through a movie without being challenged and leave everyone, from the director to the audience, satisfied. That is what one gets from watching *Up in the Air*: it is an insanely confident star turn, but akin to taking a high-powered sports car out for twenty laps on a racetrack.

The film is hamstrung by a frustrating inability to dive beneath Reitman's carefully arranged surfaces, and the director inadvertently revealed why in his interview with Indiewire's Anne Thompson: 'You know it's funny, it's not as if I'd follow George's life on *US Weekly*, and then try to punch in elements into the screenplay. I wrote a character that I thought he was perfect to play. And certainly, when he read the script for the first time he said to me, "You know, I see how people are going to draw parallels between my persona and this character, and I'm ready to stare at them straight in the eyes." I think what makes this role special for George isn't all that stuff, it's really that he shows a type of vulnerability in this film that he's never shown in any other film he's done: he's out of control. And he's particularly vulnerable in a romantic relationship. The way he is on that monorail when he's talking to Vera Farmiga, and she calls him a "parenthesis" – I hadn't seen him do that in any other movie, and he did that on day two of the shoot. I mean, he's a remarkable actor and a remarkable man. And a lot of nice things are said about him, but it's not just talk; it's actually true. He made my job easier and he made me look good.'[122] And yet there is never a moment where Clooney feels truly out of control – even in the aforementioned moment where Alex wounds him. Ryan absorbs the comment and makes the proper, conscientious adjustments to his life (e.g. surrendering his air miles to Julie and Jim). Ryan is never as stunningly vulnerable as Kelvin

is throughout the entirety of *Solaris*. He is sad and perhaps a little helpless as he stares at the airport flight chart in the final scene, but his concluding voice-over reveals a man who, at the very least, understands his dilemma. 'The stars will wheel forth from their daytime hiding places; and one of those lights, slightly brighter than the rest, will be my wingtip passing over.' There is a measure of peace in this statement. It is not a smug performance; it is just a pleasant one in a film that is too impressed with being so well organized. One problem could be that Reitman, at thirty-one, simply was not ready to delve into the anxiety of a single man nearing fifty.

Clooney, however, seems to have immensely enjoyed inhabiting the character of Ryan Bingham – largely because he got to make light of his advancing age. 'It's funny,' said Clooney, 'because most male actors work with actresses who are considerably younger. But earlier in my career I was working with a lot of actresses who were my age or older so people always thought I was older anyway; and now I'm going through this thing with people thinking I'm about 60.'[123] Clooney has arrived at the age where it is practically expected that he will get precious, if not vain, about his appearance, but he is sanguine about the ageing process. 'As you get older and ease your way into being a character actor you have to be comfortable with where you are in life and career, and I'm very comfortable with what

I'm doing – working on projects I'm proud of.'[124] Unfortunately, this comfort level infects his performance, thus blunting the impact of Bingham's heartbreaking epiphany in the final scene of the film. This is a man who will likely spend the rest of his life unmoored from a conventional family life, but is that really a tragedy? Bingham's peripatetic existence has defined him, and made him emotionally unavailable to his family (he has no long-term friends). He has emptied his backpack. There is hope for him. And yet Reitman insists on a downer conclusion. This is a movie that desperately wanted to draw blood from its star, but could not inflict so much as a paper cut.

A Fleeting Sensation

Up in the Air was rapturously reviewed by most critics, with many hailing Clooney's work as the best in his career. Writing for the *Los Angeles Times*, Kenneth Turan exclaimed, 'It's hard to think of an actor who's better at projecting the professional smoothness that's essential to make this character palatable, but Clooney turns out to be willing to take that persona further, to be both more real and more vulnerable than his charm-offensive characters are usually allowed to be.'[125] *Entertainment Weekly*'s Owen Gleiberman lavished more praise, claiming, 'In *Up in the Air*, Clooney gives his most fully felt performance to

Previous pages: Bingham invites Alex to accompany him to the wedding of his sister Julie. Here he shows her the school he attended as a child.

Above: Bingham and Alex steal a moment during an impromptu night out with Natalie.

Opposite: Daring to surprise Alex at home in Chicago, Bingham learns he is a 'parenthesis'.

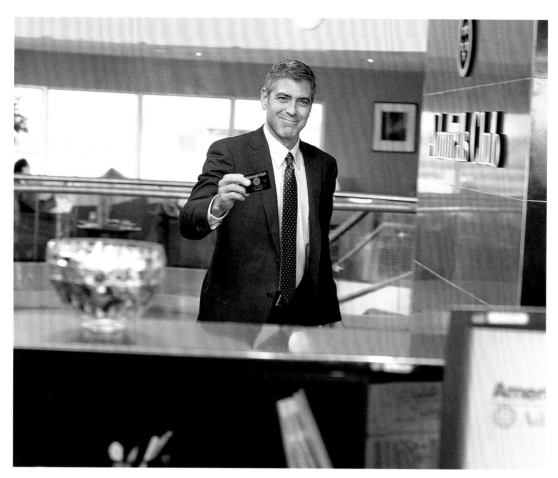

date as a smooth hedonist who comes to realize that he may be drowning. This is movie-star acting of the sort that no one else today can bring off.'[126] Even when writing a dissenting opinion, *Salon*'s Stephanie Zacharek could not help but appreciate Clooney's effort: 'And Clooney is, well, Clooney: As always, he's as silky as a pocket square (an accoutrement that, by the way, the no-frills Ryan wouldn't be caught dead in). Clooney is a marvelous actor and a great salesman – in short, he's a movie star, and hallelujah for that. He's so cashmere-casual here, he can almost make you forget how canned the language is.'[127]

But while *Up in the Air* conquered Toronto, dazzled a majority of critics and fell just short of a $100 million gross in the United States, it landed short of the Academy Awards runway. It received six nominations, including Actor in a Leading Role for Clooney, but won in no category and was not a threat to win either. The film, like Ryan, had not left an indelible impression and now stands as a reminder of how far a top-notch movie star can take ephemeral material. Still, the film is not the type to get an easy green light in Hollywood so Clooney had a point when he remarked, 'I'm not really going to survive in the studio system if all they're going to do is tentpole action films, because I'm not really that guy anymore. So my livelihood is going to depend on films like *Up in the Air* and *Goats* being successful, because if they are, we get to make more of them.'[128]

Interestingly, Clooney's most memorable 2009 performance was given in conjunction with a stop-motion canid. Wes Anderson's wonderful *Fantastic Mr. Fox* bypassed the early festivals in favour of an American Film Institute berth, and, though largely ignored by the Academy, has endured as one of the finest family films of the last decade. If anything, it is a reminder that awards buzz, even when generated by the most charismatic man on the planet, is a fickle thing.

➡️ *Fantastic Mr. Fox* (2009)

Previously, if George Clooney wanted to have some fun doing animated voice work, he would drop by *South Park* for some off-colour silliness with Trey Parker and Matt Stone. But he had never lent his voice to a feature-length animated feature until Wes Anderson came calling with his adaptation of Roald Dahl's *Fantastic Mr. Fox*. This was not to be an ordinary hang-out-in-a-recording-studio errand for Clooney: Anderson wanted the entire cast to record in barns and forests and old houses in the London countryside. 'I was excited about the whole process,' said Clooney, 'and I think it was a very different process from what most people go through when they work on an animated film. We were out in the middle of nowhere, on people's farms, and doing sound effects and rolling around in the fields – so it was fun to do.'[y]

'Fun' was the order of the day, and the actors threw themselves into their voice work with a physical abandon that is rare for animated moviemaking. 'We spent the night sleeping out [in a farmhouse] and running around in these barns. We didn't have a wolf yet and Bill [Murray] acted out the part of the wolf… I don't know about other animated films, but I don't think you usually get the chance to work with all the other guys, and it was like going to camp.'[z] Combined with the handmade vibe of the stop-motion animation, *Fantastic Mr. Fox* turned out to be a wonderfully authentic and, ultimately, poignant family film. Though Clooney's titular character is a thief who routinely endangers his family by pilfering food, he is also a devoted father who must make peace with his artistically inclined son's disinterest in athletics and all

the spry exploits for which foxes are famous. Clooney did not just provide a voice to Anderson's film; he gave him his heart.

Jack/Edward

9

The American** (2010)
Anton Corbijn

'I'm no good with machines.'
—Jack

Many years ago, before Section Eight and
his subsequent production ventures, Clooney
professed a love for Jonathan Glazer's *Sexy Beast*.
It was his favourite movie of 2000, which stands
out insofar as Clooney's personal taste is concerned
for its recklessness, absurdity and unapologetic
cruelty. Until 2010, that was a type of film
Clooney had not come close to making; moreover,
it does not feel like he would have the DNA for
that kind of movie. *Sexy Beast* is dominated
by a sociopath whose every other word is 'fuck'
or 'cunt'; he is such a vile and savage man, that
the viewer cannot help but laugh at his awfulness.
He is a flesh-and-blood cartoon. Maybe that is
why Clooney, *South Park*'s friend and former
benefactor, loves it; that is all very well, but
would he ever have the chutzpah to place
himself in the centre of a film that is so cheerfully
nihilistic? Back in the early days of Section Eight,
Soderbergh recalls meeting with directors who
trafficked in darker sensibilities: 'I remember we
very much wanted to work with Jonathan Glazer.
We wanted to work with David Lynch. We went
down the list of people we liked and just called
them up and said, "Is there anything you're doing
that we can help get going?"'[129]

The idea of Clooney in a Lynch film is a brain-
melter, to say the least. There is, however, an
untapped perversity in Clooney that is hinted at
in the Coens' *Burn After Reading*, but that is just
a vague notion. Letting this very polished but game
charmer loose in a sexually charged nightmare
is the kind of daring idea that, of his movie-star
forebears, only James Stewart seriously entertained
(in *Vertigo*, 1958). Ever since his early stumbles,
Clooney has taken mostly calculated risks; *Solaris*
was a flop, but it was pedigreed and, sexually, a
Sunday sermon compared to *Blue Velvet* (1986).
What a kinky blast it would be to see Clooney give
himself, and his image, over to a twisted genius
like Lynch – or imagine him as one of Scarlett
Johansson's victims in Glazer's *Under the Skin*
(2013). Emasculating himself, or risking complete
embarrassment, is the one thing Clooney has not
openly entertained. The closest he has come to
denting his reputation as a mensch, to playing a bad
man for keeps, is in Anton Corbijn's *The American*.

The Hired Gun

Based on the 1990 novel *A Very Private Gentleman*
by Martin Booth, *The American* is a highly
unusual project for Clooney in a number of ways,
starting with the choice of director. Born in the
Netherlands in 1955, Corbijn developed his
visual talents as a photographer, documenting
the post-punk and new wave music scene in the
late 1970s and early '80s. His work has graced the
covers of many rock albums, most notably those
of U2 and Depeche Mode, with whom he has
enjoyed a long and highly influential collaboration.
Like Glazer, Corbijn also dabbled in music videos,
directing 'One' for U2, 'Never Let Me Down
Again' for Depeche Mode and 'Heart-Shaped
Box' for Nirvana (the band's last official video).
He finally segued into features in 2007 with
Control, a critically acclaimed biopic about
Joy Division frontman Ian Curtis. Like many
in-demand filmmakers, Corbijn was courted by
studios and movie stars eager to align themselves
with (or simply exploit) a *sui generis* aesthetic that
might confer some manner of artistic integrity
on their work, but the opportunity to team with
Clooney (a mutual friend of Bono's) turned out
to be the right fit post-*Control*. 'He's only done
one movie,' said Clooney, 'and it was great, and
that's not always the case with guys who have
done music videos. A lot of the times they don't
know how to tell a complete story, but he's very
talented and I'm very excited to be working with
him.'[130] In light of Clooney's stated reticence for
working with first-time directors, it is curious that
he was not put off by Corbijn's admission of his
inexperience: 'I didn't really know how to make
a film when I made *Control*. I had to create my
own language, just as I did when I started taking
photographs. I never studied either one.'[131]

Rowan Joffe adapted the book, changing the
nationality of the titular gentleman from English
to American. Corbijn explained the essence of the
film: 'So I looked at thrillers, dark comedies, all
these things I could see in myself. I found something
I could invest myself in, the question in the film
is really if a man can really change his life. It's
the core of the film. And it's about a loner just as
Control was about a loner.'[132] Clooney had played
a loner of sorts just a year earlier in *Up in the Air*,
but this was an altogether different type of man.

Jack/Edward, the professional
killer played by Clooney
in the Anton Corbijn film
The American (2010).

Jack is a hired gunman; he kills for a living and
evinces zero compunction about putting a bullet
in anyone's brain. In the film's first scene, Jack's
romantic getaway with his lover is interrupted
when he senses he is being tracked; his instincts
are correct and he shoots the gunman in front of
the stunned woman, who clearly knows nothing
of his life. Whether worried that his cover is blown
or suspicious that she might have led him into
an ambush, Jack murders her without hesitation.
In just a matter of minutes, Jack's warm, romantic
facade has crumbled to reveal a remorseless,
practically expressionless killer. It is the most
ruthless act committed by Clooney in a film since
The Peacemaker, where he gunned down a couple
of helpless villains in a disabled car; one could
point back to the butchery of *From Dusk Till
Dawn*, but that is all carried off with a smirk.
This is real, cold-blooded murder, and Corbijn's
film only goes so far to humanize this predator.

The Clothes Make The Killer

'George was into it, which surprised me', Corbijn
told *The Guardian* in 2010. 'Maybe it's because
he's never played such a dark character. Perhaps in
Michael Clayton or *Syriana* he was unsympathetic,
but he's never been this harsh or unappealing.
It was fabulous for me that he was able to go
that dark. He does so much with so little. He was
ideal.'[133] Visually and narratively, Corbijn follows
Clooney's lead with beautifully framed widescreen
compositions that soak in the gorgeous Italian
scenery; the director tips his hand during a
moment in a small restaurant, where a scene
from Sergio Leone's *Once Upon a Time in the
West* (1968) can be glimpsed. But it is not an
empty homage: the scene in question features
Henry Fonda, whose villain in Leone's classic
was jarring for a generation of filmgoers who had
grown up knowing him as such morally upright
characters as Abraham Lincoln and Wyatt Earp.
Clooney's murder of the woman at the outset of
The American does not carry that kind of power
(there is no Ennio Morricone score and Clooney
does not kill an unarmed child), but it is the same
kind of image tinkering.

For Corbijn, it was not just about finding
the dark corners of Clooney's psyche, it was also
crucial to tap into the actor's well-known rage
and sculpt it into something truly unnerving.
'I liked it when he was angry in *Michael Clayton*
and I liked *Syriana*', says Corbijn. 'These are the
references for me in his work… the ones that
I like. So, I wanted to continue with that anger.
But this is definitely his darkest role to date as
well as one of his finest performances, in my
opinion. But I could see he could do that and
I really enjoyed bringing that out in him, especially
because you don't normally get to see it. It's more
often this charming man, which he naturally is.
But this goes against the grain almost.'[134]

This makes it one of the most unusual films in Clooney's oeuvre; as written, the character gives him zero opportunity to fall back on his charisma. It is by far the deepest Clooney has ever sunk into a character, and this is all the more impressive because, according to Corbijn, Clooney could slip in and out of character as smoothly as putting on and taking off a jacket.

However, while Corbijn succeeded in eliciting a brooding performance from Clooney, the shooting of the film was hardly a dreary experience. Even when playing a contract killer, Clooney has got to blow off a little steam with on-set practical jokes. 'I made a book of the film called *Inside The American*,' says Corbijn, 'so I had a camera on set but there were days that I had no time whatsoever to take snapshots. My camera was always on my chair, though, and at one point I got the films back and I remember thinking: "I never saw these pictures! I can't recall them." Then there was someone's naked butt. But then I realized it was George's because I recognized the T-shirt. He had taken my camera and asked his assistant to take pictures of his naked butt.'[135]

Since Clooney is not his usual gregarious self in *The American*, it fell upon the costume designer, Suttirat Anne Larlarb (best known for her long association with Danny Boyle), to accentuate the actor's subtle performance with some exceptionally stylish threads. 'To have someone like George Clooney playing such a character for me meant

stripping away from him anything that was glamorous or fashion forward. It was very necessary to normalize him, especially because we were not in a fashion-forward city like Rome or Milan. He has picked a small town with 75-year-old men sitting on benches drinking their cappuccinos; he has to blend into that. But, at the same time, Jack is played by one of the best-dressed men on the planet, and we didn't want to strip him of his handsomeness and individuality. It was a balance. […] George is very smart. […] He knew his character had to blend in. We went with timeless classics – nothing branded or slick. The only kind of high design was his final suit at the end of the movie. He has to acquire a suit for a procession, and in all these towns that's where you wear your Sunday finest.'[136] For a minimalist film like *The American*, details like costume design matter more than most: the clothes not only make the man, they give one a sense of the character's inner life. He is blending in, sure, but this is an outsider's idea of 'blending in'; this is what Jack thinks is normal, and it is as much a giveaway as bumbling around in an 'I Love Italy' T-shirt with a Fodor's guidebook tucked under his arm. He is antisocial by necessity. He does not belong anywhere. He will sit with the village priest for a glass of brandy, but will betray no enjoyment. As the priest asks Jack about his past and his purpose in this part of the country, Jack offers terse answers; his head remains static (TV George

is dead), but his eyes move left to right as if looking for an exit. Killing is second nature, but socializing? This is the worst part of his job.

As Jack holes up in the mountain village of Castelvecchio, assembling a custom-built rifle for a beautiful fellow assassin named Mathilde (Thekla Reuten), he downplays his presence and tries to keep to himself. (Clooney was especially fond of shooting in the small town. According to Corbijn, 'After filming he told me it was his favourite location ever because he could walk around there without anybody noticing him and he hadn't had that for eighteen years.'¹³⁷ But while anonymity was delightful for Clooney, it is a survival instinct for Jack – something to be ferociously guarded, not savoured.) However, he soon falls for Clara (Violante Placido), a prostitute who elicits both genuine love and suspicion; Jack has not survived this long without considering that everyone unfortunate enough to enter his orbit might have designs on snuffing him out, and he does not spare Clara from such consideration. Like Leone's spaghetti westerns, Corbijn is giving into convention, which is fine, but he does not possess the Italian maestro's interest in staging operatic set pieces. And so the film becomes a narratively and visually spare meditation on redemption, with the tragic outcome utterly predetermined. The only way Jack gets out of this alive is if he severs ties with Clara completely, which would essentially require a cold-blooded

echo of the film's opening scene. It would be fascinating to see Clooney go there, but this would be one step too far for a beloved movie star of his stature; if he is going to play a stone-cold killer, he has ultimately got to answer for his sins. But this is still the most menacing character he has ever allowed himself to play, and one of the few times he has allowed himself to die on screen. It is a significant departure, and a performance that demands re-evaluation, especially for those who find Clooney more smug than charming. Clooney needs to get out of his comfort zone more often, and challenge himself to do more than work minor variations on Newman's unglamorous work in *The Verdict*. He must – in a fictional sense, of course – kill again.

Not American Enough

For an aggressively uncommercial film lacking much in the way of action, *The American* did surprisingly good business in the United States. Interestingly, it was the first movie in years to be sold exclusively on Clooney's presence, and it opened to a respectable $13 million gross. The film did not travel well, but it was successful enough to recoup on its reported $20 million budget (Clooney, once again, took a sizeable pay cut to get the picture made). That is impressive for a movie with one major star, one significant set piece and a 'D' from CinemaScore.

Above: Jack and Mathilde (Thekla Reuten) test out a rebuilt rifle.

Opposite: US President Barack Obama meets in 2009 with actor George Clooney in the Oval Office during his first 100 Days in Office.

Following pages: Clara (Violante Placido) shares a moment of near-tenderness with Jack.

Optics have been key to political success in the United States, ever since Republican vice presidential candidate Richard Nixon gave his famous 'Checkers speech' in 1952 (a lesson he quickly forgot when he sweated his way through a 1960 presidential debate with the highly telegenic John F. Kennedy). Americans like candidates who project strength, who stand ready to defend their country against all enemies; they thrill to genuine-seeming rhetoric, especially when it is delivered forcefully and articulately. Whether they want to admit it or not, they are looking for movie stars to do for them in real life what they do for the world on the big screen – and when given the chance to vote for one, they often cannot resist.

George Clooney has not shied from politics in his personal life: he vigorously supported Barack Obama in two successful presidential campaigns, he came to his father's aid when he ran (unsuccessfully) for the Kentucky Senate, and he has pressured the United Nations to act against the ongoing genocide in the Sudan. So why has he not followed in the footsteps of Ronald Reagan, Clint Eastwood and even Warren Beatty (who flirted with a presidential run in 1999)? He is more polished and (with the arguable exception of Beatty) more handsome than those men, and he could potentially carry a number of Midwestern swing states as a son of the region. Unfortunately, the person most against a George Clooney run for office is George Clooney: 'I'd be such a terrible candidate. I have absolutely no patience for compromise. Famous people don't have to compromise very often; politicians have to compromise all the time. It would make me crazy. You want to get some appropriation bill through, and you're going to have to build a bridge in Alaska to do it? I'd go nuts."[aa]

Critically, the movie had its defenders, with Roger Ebert's four-star review providing cover fire against the detractors. 'There is not a wrong shot', said Ebert. 'Every performance is tightly controlled. Clooney is in complete command of his effect. He sometimes seems to be chewing a very small piece of gum, or perhaps his tongue.'[138] But *The New York Times*'s A.O. Scott was not sold at all: 'Mr. Clooney, shorn of his mischief and charm, does not possess the resources to suggest the state of existential torment that are crucial to the logic of his character. Instead he looks bored, tired, intermittently anxious and sometimes almost excited. At least he seems to appreciate the beauty of the scenery, human and otherwise. It's hard not to when so little else is going on.'[139] *Variety*'s Robert Koehler got it right, however, by noting, 'Clooney may not have a hit this time, but he continues to apply considerable intelligence to his work as an actor, still trying to deliver something fresh and interesting for his fans. This is undeniably his movie, though Leysen as the distanced boss projects a mysterious malice.'[140]

Corbijn understood the disconnect, blaming the trailer for selling a more exciting movie than the deliberately paced one he had made. An amused Corbijn commented: 'A lot of critics were angry. The trailer made it look like it was one thing – a fast-paced, popcorn, Hollywood thriller – when it was something else entirely. So when they got into the screenings and found that it was a European take on a western, they were furious.'[141] There was probably never a big audience for this movie. Though the sight of a silver-haired Clooney doing a murderous homage to Lee Marvin is enough to get any cinephile's engine running, the film does not have a clever twist or a conventional emotional hook to draw in mainstream moviegoers. It is undeniably an art film: as much in thrall to the films of Michelangelo Antonioni as it is to Leone. Clooney did very little in the way of promotion for *The American*; typically, there would be at least one magazine cover profile pegged to a new film from this particular movie star, but he sat this cycle out. Clooney has never gone on record disowning *The American*, but he has not exactly stuck up for it either; meanwhile, the choices he has made in the wake of the film's release suggest he is not eager to head back down the bumpy road to experimentation. Perhaps he was conscious of the need to rebuild a bit of goodwill with his audience. If so, Clooney was to accomplish that the following year by ticking off yet another major filmmaker from his 'To Collaborate With' list.

Betrayal and escape. Jack flees, but not before being mortally wounded.

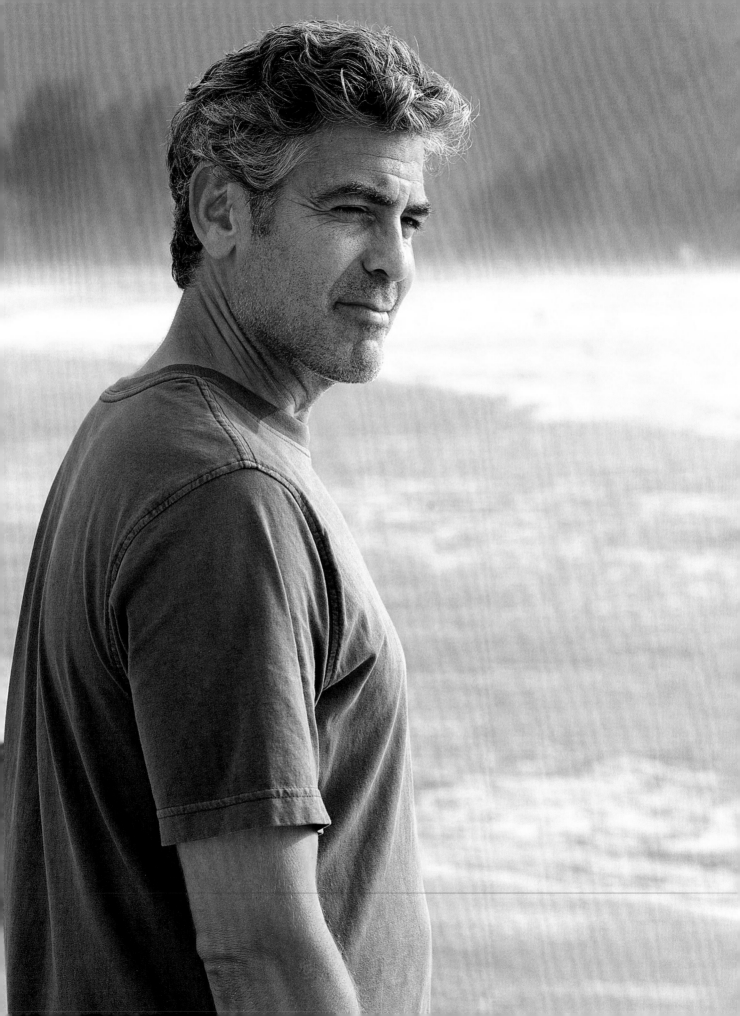

10

Matt King

The Descendants (2011)
Alexander Payne

'I'm the backup parent. The understudy.'
—Matt King

In 2011, Clooney, like many a human being before him, turned fifty, thus reaching the age where normal people could disgustedly clutch their pot belly, or clutch at their jowls or frown at their crow's feet and wonder what Faustian genetic bargain this movie star had struck to so glamorously look his age. Here is a guy who, two years before, was fretting that he might have to start wearing make-up in front of the camera, thereby reminding the general public that he did not need any kind of concealment to mask the ravages of age. He was not the first actor to thrust a middle finger at the passage of time: in 1977 a fifty-two-year-old Paul Newman laced up the skates and took to the ice in the boisterously brilliant *Slap Shot*. Clooney matches up remarkably well to his acting idol; though he does not possess a solitary feature as miraculous as Newman's piercing blue eyes, he appears to be better preserved and still having a high time making movies. He is aware of mortality, but his phobias are predictably centred on an involuntary curtailment of his work ethic: 'I'm terrified of dying and having not accomplished the things that I want to do', he told *The Hollywood Reporter*. 'I am terrified of not finishing, or at least not participating enough. Everybody has a fear of death, but my fear isn't dying; it's of not getting the job done.'[142]

However, productivity was hardly an issue for Clooney. Heading into an 'on' year in 2011, he had his fourth directorial effort in *The Ides of March* and a plum starring role as a distressed dad in Alexander Payne's *The Descendants* (the filmmaker's first feature since *Sideways* in 2004). On another exciting note, he had managed to get himself arrested while protesting outside of the Sudanese Embassy in Washington, DC. Joining him in the cells was his father, Nick, who at seventy-seven had to be proud of his son's unswerving devotion to speaking up for those less powerful and fortunate than him. These were the noble beliefs instilled in the young George, the child that once bit a dog back for biting him. In both the political and cinematic arena, the son had honoured his upbringing – though a spanking might still be in order for *Batman & Robin*.

Et Tu, Kentucky?

The acrid aftertaste of his father's unsuccessful campaign for a Kentucky seat in the US House of Representatives lingered in the younger Clooney's craw like the spinal fluid he coughed up on the set of *Syriana* – in part because he knew his involvement had hastened the old man's defeat. In an interview with his hometown newspaper, *The Cincinnati Enquirer*, Clooney said his father had branded the experience 'uncomfortable, embarrassing and at times humiliating'.[143] So it is no surprise that Clooney took to Beau Willimon's *Farragut North*, a stage play based on the writer's frustrating experiences as a volunteer for Howard Dean's 2004 presidential bid. *The Ides of March* is a spiky and cynical examination of an idealistic press secretary (Ryan Gosling) who comes to learn that the charismatic presidential candidate (George Clooney) for whom he is stumping is not quite the Great Man he believes him to be. Clooney and Grant Heslov transplanted the main action of Willimon's drama to Ohio, but retained the dour tone. 'We were working on a morality play', said Clooney. 'We had a couple of different versions of it, basically about "Do the ends justify the means? And at what point is it OK to sell your soul?"'[144] Clooney cited as an inspiration the films of the 1960s and '70s that he grew up loving, and there are clear echoes of everything from *The Candidate* (1972) to *All the President's Men* (1976) in the movie. *The Ides of March* is an effective political thriller, despite the narrative tripping up over an unnecessarily overblown tragedy in the third act. Over the next few years it became clear that Clooney preferred directing to acting, but if he was already feeling bored with the on-camera rigmarole, it did not show in his other 2011 movie.

Father Knows Nothing

For an actor who is so meticulous and deliberate in how he chooses projects, it is telling that Clooney's only portrayal of a (relatively) happily married man was in *Fantastic Mr. Fox*. Normally when he plays a father it is a divorcee whose children either hate his guts or barely know him (with the forgettable *One Fine Day* serving as the nitpicker's exception to the rule). To what extent

Clooney chose to play Matt King, a father of two soon-to-be-motherless daughters, in Alexander Payne's *The Descendants* (2011).

With the director Alexander Payne, who hoped to elicit a more emotionally grounded performance from his star.

Opposite: Learning that his currently comatose wife, Elizabeth, had a lover, Matt makes a panicked sprint to his friends' house to get the full, sordid truth.

Following pages: Payne decided to focus in his script on the relationship between Matt and his older daughter, Alex (Shailene Woodley).

this is intentional is hard to say; Clooney is the product of a loving Catholic household and he obviously maintains a great relationship with his father to this day. But in his own adult life as Hollywood's most eligible bachelor, the closest he has come to fatherhood is having a pet (the infamous pot-bellied pig, Max, or his rescue pup, Einstein). He has expressed no particular yearning for children, and only recently took himself off the marriage market, so his penchant for playing messed-up dads is curious.

On a more predictable note, Clooney's tendency to work with the most distinctive voices in modern cinema led him to pursue Alexander Payne for the better part of a decade, dating at least as far back as *Sideways*. Clooney lobbied to play the role of Jack, the struggling television actor whose shot at stardom has come and gone, but Payne opted for Thomas Haden Church. 'I wouldn't believe the most handsome and successful movie actor playing the most washed-up TV actor', said Payne. 'I didn't want that to be the joke.'[145] But when Payne re-emerged seven years later with *The Descendants*, featuring the lead character of Matt King, a father struggling to raise two daughters as his wife lies comatose in a hospital, the filmmaker thought Clooney seemed a perfect fit. 'He's right for *The Descendants* because he's the right age, he's the right look – one of those handsome rich guys out in Hawaii. And also emotionally [right] for the part – because

we film viewers have detected in Clooney's work a certain charming detachment from emotions… how he looks at the proceedings going on around him with a certain twinkle in his eye… I thought that would be accurate for the character of someone who's grown detached from the emotions of his own life, and has to grow to be more connected and aware and in touch with his own feelings.'[146] This is solid rationale for casting Clooney and yet a little disappointing, as anyone who has seen *Solaris* would have a hard time saying the actor has always evinced a 'charming detachment from emotions'.

Clooney was thrilled for the opportunity to finally collaborate with Payne, the Nebraska-born satirist (though, perhaps in a bit of a good-natured nudge for the previous casting slight, he did ask to read the script first). The two men are not a great deal alike in public (Payne can be prickly, while Clooney is, as Stephanie Zacharek once said, 'Clooney'), but their Midwest upbringings unite their sensibilities; they are men who appreciate and understand the folks back home, while also knowing full well how authentically silly they can be. This accords well with Clooney's image-tweaking: Matt King is not a Coen-level goofball, but he is a middle-aged man who is oblivious to much of what is going on with his children and his wife. According to Clooney, 'I just have to share getting older with everybody in the world on screen and it's a little trickier, but I'm OK with

Matt informs Alex that her mother will never emerge from her coma and that it is time to remove her from life support.

Opposite: Matt and Alex must make peace; Elizabeth's (Patricia Hastie) impending death; and an inescapable lack of resolution.

Following pages: Matt and his daughters are joined by Alex's oddball friend Sid (Nick Krause) as they head to Kauai to confront Elizabeth's lover, Brian.

it. I felt this was a good place to talk about fears and loss in your life and Alexander Payne was the perfect director to do it with. In this film I got to rediscover what it was like to not be confident.'[147]

Fuck Paradise

Based on a novel by Kaui Hart Hemmings, *The Descendants* began its movie life as an adaptation by the screenwriting duo of Jim Rash and Nat Faxon. Payne had optioned the book to produce, but was working on another script with his writing partner Jim Taylor; when he finally decided to direct the film himself in 2009, he tapped out his own adaptation, which differed significantly from the book and the Rash/Faxon draft. Payne explained, 'Both the book and their adaptation had a lot more to do with the younger daughter, with Scottie. I was far less interested in her than I was the man's relationship with the older daughter. Plus, as a director, I know when you work with minors, you only have eight hours per day to work with them, and who needs that?'[148] By placing Matt King front and centre, and punching up the part of seventeen-year-old Alex (Shailene Woodley), Payne gifted Clooney with a chance to try on big-screen parenthood for, essentially, the first time. A successful Honolulu lawyer, Matt is on the cusp of selling a family-controlled 25,000 acres of prime real estate on Kauai Island. As Matt scrambles to negotiate the

best deal (the family's trust is set to expire in seven years), he must also contend with his hospitalized wife, Elizabeth (Patricia Hastie), who is on a life-support machine after a boating accident. When Elizabeth's doctor informs Matt that her death is not a question of 'if, but when', he summons a drug-addled Alex from her boarding school on the Big Island so that she can say goodbye to her mother. Further complicating matters is Matt's youngest daughter, Scottie (Amara Miller), who has taken to beating up her classmates. Matt is paying a price for being an aloof father – and if this was not trouble enough, Alex shatters his world by revealing that Elizabeth was carrying on an affair with real estate agent Brian Speer (Matthew Lillard). Once Matt processes this, he resolves to visit Brian and invite him to bid farewell to Elizabeth (who loved him) – only to find that Brian is happily married and, even worse, did not share Elizabeth's affections.

Watching Clooney come to terms with being the cheated-upon party in an affair is a jarring change of pace, and he looks the part. Clad in gaudy Hawaiian shirts, shorts and flip-flops, he comes off as a style icon for burned-out beach bums; he is also sporting a wavy clump of hair that gives him the appearance of *Hawaii Five-O*'s Jack Lord gone grey. It is hideous stuff, but it is in keeping with the quotidian garishness that makes Honolulu as drab in its way as Omaha. 'It's not a story about tourists', explains Payne. 'It's a story

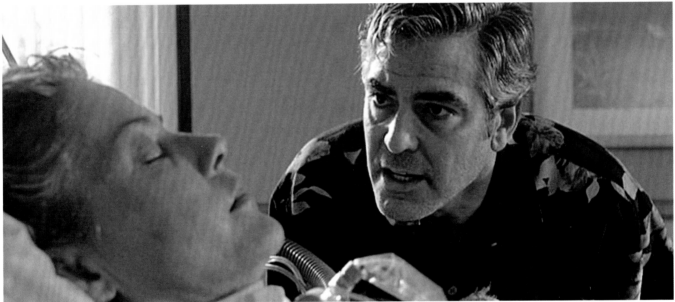

Gravity (2013)

George Clooney has never seemed more right for a part than Matt Kowalski in Alfonso Cuarón's *Gravity*. The feeling is mutual for Cuarón, who found Clooney to be a valuable collaborator both on screen and off. 'We've been approaching each other to work together for years, and it was almost like something that completely made sense. And George is a terrific actor, an amazing writer, and a gifted director. So he gets it. He's concerned not just about his scenes, but the film.'[bb] Clooney's versatility was especially helpful in improving the screenplay. 'There was one scene we were doing over and over and over, and George overheard that we were dealing with that. And then one night I receive an e-mail from him, saying, "I heard you were struggling with this. I took a shot with the scene. Read it. Throw it out." And we ended up using it. This was exactly what we needed.'[cc]

As a loquacious, laid-back astronaut casually guiding Ryan Stone (Sandra Bullock) through her first space mission (a spacewalk to perform routine maintenance on the Hubble Space Telescope), Clooney emits a good old boy charm swiped from Dennis Quaid's Gordo Cooper in *The Right Stuff* (1983). He is keeping it light, kicking back to Hank Williams Jr's 'Angels Are Hard to Find' and gently assuaging Stone's anxiety – which is considerable. But while he is genuinely enjoying what is to be his last space jaunt, he is also aware that catastrophes happen when tensions run high. And when a catastrophe occurs while orbiting the Earth, there is very little chance of survival. This point is made to thrilling effect in the film's first ten minutes, as debris from an exploded Russian satellite pelts the Hubble and the team's shuttle. Within minutes, Stone is spinning off into deep space, and the ride home is irreparably disabled. It is up to veteran Kowalski to save the day: he pulls Stone out of her spiral and gets her to the International Space Station. However, Stone's survival becomes a solo mission once Kowalski helplessly drifts away from the ISS; aside from a hallucinatory conversation in a spacecraft,

Gravity is Bullock's show. *Gravity* is significant in Clooney's oeuvre in that it allows him to tick off his 'to work with' list another world-class auteur. In doing press for the film, Clooney went out of his way to give his collaborators the spotlight: '[Sandra's] so good in the movie. I think it's gonna be a beautiful, beautiful film. But it's a big risk. To have Alfonso basically saying, "I'm gonna put you guys in space suits and make this a story about survival and really about your own sort of personal journey." I think it's a very brave film. I love, love, love, love Alfonso. There's a guy who truly is an artist.'[dd]

Opposite: *Gravity* (2013) by Alfonso Cuarón. Clooney offers superb support to co-star Sandra Bullock.

Above: The father and his two daughters, Alex and Scottie (Amara Miller), enjoy ice cream at the end of a long, strange journey.

about people who live there, so that point of view comes automatically with the story. I wasn't wishing to evoke anything. There's a bit of a joke made at the beginning of the film, "Paradise can go fuck itself". The voice-over and the images tell the viewer right off the bat, "You're going to be seeing a different side of what you consider Hawaii."'[149] Clooney's never been afraid of dishevelment, but his outfits in *The Descendants* represent deafening bad taste. This is amusingly complemented by a cloddish physical bearing that allows him to work a hilarious variation on the funny walk: after learning of Elizabeth's infidelity, he sprints down the street to his friends' house to interrogate them about what they knew; along the way, he has to navigate a long curve in the road, which Payne captures in a single full-shot for maximum awkwardness. When Payne cuts to Clooney's face, the actor conveys an alarming mixture of panic and exertion; it is as if Matt is confronting his mortality with each thudding stride. That Matt's awful hair keeps getting more messed up as the film wears on completes the picture of a man in an emotional tailspin – and Clooney locks into the character with an authentic befuddlement that is essentially Ulysses Everett McGill dialled back from eleven to, at most, two. 'He has an amazing range and technical craft', said Payne. 'He'll maintain his emotions and intensity while adjusting his head 4.5 degrees this way or that.'[150] For the much

younger Woodley, any potential of being overwhelmed by Clooney vanished immediately. 'George Clooney sort of lost his "George Clooney-ness" the first day I met him', she told *Vulture*. 'He's not George Clooney in my eyes – he's George from Kentucky with an awesome, awesome heart.'[151]

Clooney's performance contains some of the most nuanced character work he has ever turned in; underneath the gaudy exterior, one can trace Matt's emotional journey from obliviousness to complete emotional engagement. Early in the film, when he retrieves a resentful Alex from her boarding school, he seeks her help in dealing with Scottie's burgeoning delinquency. Given her drug use, Alex seems a questionable parental substitute, but Matt is clueless. Clooney gets this across beautifully in the scene where Alex, newly returned from school, goes for a swim in their unkempt pool (yet another sign of Matt's spiritual turmoil). He is practically reaching out to her with his pleading words as he walks along the side of the water, but nothing is landing; he seems diminished, dominated. But in the later scenes at the hospital, before the family bids farewell to their comatose mother, Clooney has bridged the gap with Woodley, standing a little straighter and comfortably inhabiting the same frame with her. These are the small moves Payne spoke of, and they are seismic in terms of their emotional impact. 'I enjoyed playing the character but I don't know that I can relate to him', he said. 'But part of my job is to do what is asked of me in the script and not have to worry about whether it pertains to me or not. You don't have to actually shoot heroin to play a drug addict, you know.'[152] This is fascinating because it is not until late in the film that Matt seems to truly relate to Alex and Scottie – and even then he is a bit of a dork. But in the film's final scene, with the three remaining Kings eating ice cream while draped under Elizabeth's quilt, there is a genuine connection between a once-distant father and his distraught children. But it is Matt who looks at home playing papa, not Clooney. When Payne called cut, one can easily imagine the dapper charmer coming out to play and cracking self-deprecating jokes about his wardrobe; but in the moment, there is no George Clooney, just Matt King.

A Schlemiel in Full

The Descendants débuted at the 2011 Telluride Film Festival, and rode a wave of critical euphoria through the entirety of the awards season. *The Hollywood Reporter*'s Todd McCarthy got the rave tour started two months before the film's theatrical release, singling out Clooney and Woodley for their excellent performances. 'But it's Clooney who carries it all with an underplayed, sometimes self-deprecating and exceptionally resonant performance. He's onscreen nearly all the time (and narrates as well) and makes it easy to spend nearly two hours with a man forced to carry more than his fair share of the weight of the world on his shoulders for a spell.'[153] This was echoed by *The Washington Post*'s Ann Hornaday, who effused, 'Eschewing his movie-star glamour without once shedding his compulsive watchability, Clooney moves through all those feelings in his best, most complex performance since *Michael Clayton*.'[154] But there were those who felt Payne's drama sounded a false note, finding fault with the picture's on-the-nose voice-over and laying the blame for the movie's perceived inauthenticity at its star's open-toed sandals. 'Clooney, like Angelina Jolie, may be becoming a prisoner of his own Olympian looks and fame', carped *Slate*'s Dana Stevens. 'Even shambling around in shorts, flip-flops, and a goofy floral shirt, this man is self-evidently not a schlemiel.'[155]

Unlike 2009's *Up in the Air*, *The Descendants* paced itself throughout awards season and garnered five Academy Award nominations, with Payne, Faxon and Rash winning for Best Adapted Screenplay (beating Clooney, Heslov and Willimon for *The Ides of March*). Clooney was viewed as a frontrunner for Best Actor in early fall, but Jean Dujardin gradually dominated the race for his expressive performance in Michel Hazanavicius's silent film, *The Artist*. Clooney expressed only admiration for Dujardin, going so far as to cast the French actor two years later in his fifth directorial work, *The Monuments Men* (2014). Again, if Clooney was concerned about anything, it was squandering whatever time he has left on this planet. 'My biggest fear is doing the same things 10 years from now', he said. 'That would be a failure. It's something you have to constantly reassess, and asking yourself what you are going to do next makes it a good, long full journey.'[156] Since *The Descendants*, he has appeared in only three movies: a supporting role in *Gravity* (2013), the lead of an ensemble cast in *The Monuments Men*, and in *Tomorrowland* (2015). The 'on' year/'off' year rhythm has been broken, which lends credence to the notion that he might be phasing out of acting – or, at least, acting as his primary career. There is also the none-too-minor fact that he was married to lawyer Amal Alamuddin in 2014. There was a time when this was considered unthinkable, but now it felt vaguely right. Clooney has always had impeccable timing.

In letting go of Elizabeth, Matt earns solace and the love of his daughters.

Conclusion

On the evening of 11 January 2015, George Clooney received the Cecil B. DeMille Award for lifetime achievement from the Hollywood Foreign Press. There was an appropriately cheeky introduction from his friends Julianna Margulies and Don Cheadle, followed by a highlight reel of moments from his best films (many a snark-drunk Twitterer bemoaned the absence of a *Facts of Life* snippet) and then a speech. Clooney opened with a joke about the Sony hacking scandal, putting the room – and, by extension, the entire industry – briefly at ease over the illegal leaking of emails that confirmed outsiders' suspicions about Hollywood being a cut-throat town run by out-of-touch white people. He told Amal Alamuddin that he was 'proud' to be her husband (thereby acknowledging her international stature and astonishing personal achievements), and then, in what at first appeared to be a misstep, began patting his peers on the back for being special. But this would not be a reprise of his misjudged 2006 Oscar speech; it was something far more graceful, and, most importantly, Clooney-esque.

'For the record: If you are in this room, you've caught the brass ring. You get to do what you've always dreamed to do and be celebrated for it, and that just… it ain't losing. I don't remember what awards Lauren Bacall won. I just remember her saying, "You know how to whistle, Steve? You just put your lips together and blow." And I have no idea what kind of hardware Robin Williams took home. But I sure remember "carpe diem" and, "Seize the day, boys. Make your lives extraordinary." I never forget that.'[157]

Throughout his career, Clooney has hit the same notes: he fought hard to earn the stardom many filmmakers and producers and executives felt was rightfully his, and he is goddamn lucky to have succeeded beyond his wildest dreams. He is a man who lives to be on set making movies, who does not wall himself off in his trailer, who makes sure everyone – from the craft services employees to the kid pulling cables to the security guard keeping watch over luxury cars that cost more than he has made in maybe three years – feels appreciated. This is why, when people go digging for dirt on George Clooney, they generally wind up covered in their own filth. 'He's just such a good friend', says Soderbergh. 'He's the guy you want next to you when you go to war. If you had

500 of them you could take over a country. You'd *lose* it within weeks because of all the partying, but you'd be able to take it over.'[158]

Clooney definitely is not getting timid in his advancing years; in September 2014 it was announced that he would direct an adaptation of journalist Nick Davies's *Hack Attack: The Inside Story of How the Truth Caught Up with Rupert Murdoch*. Yes, that's News Corp's Rupert Murdoch, and, yes, it's an examination of the phone-hacking scandal that brought down the 168-year-old *News of the World*. Clooney has once again been drawn back to his father's profession and, unlike *Good Night, and Good Luck*, this time he is going to take on a man who is still very much alive and very much in power. Clooney could not sound more thrilled. 'This has all the elements – lying, corruption, blackmail – at the highest levels of government by the biggest newspaper in London', said Clooney. 'And the fact that it's true is the best part. Nick is a brave and stubborn reporter and we consider it an honour to put his book to film.'[159]

Clooney still loves a good scrap, and why wouldn't he? He is yet to be humiliated or diminished by scandal, and he only seems to attract more admirers when he stands up to the world's bullies. It is difficult not to lapse into hagiography with Clooney but, given what is currently on the record regarding his private life, if one were to make The George Clooney Story as a movie, it would invariably depict the actor as the guy everyone would like to grab a drink with. According to Soderbergh, 'If you were to talk to anybody who's remotely close to him… he's the most generous person I've ever met. He's the world's best host. If everybody's not having a good time, then he's not having a good time. He has an enormous capacity for friendship. He's so loyal. He values his friendships, makes them a priority – and he would be this way regardless.'[160] George Clooney is not 'The Next Cary Grant', nor is he 'The Last Movie Star'; he is just a conscientious guy who was brought up right by his parents and put in the work to get where he is today. It is the disgustingly perfect story of a man who knows he is handsome and who has spent the last thirty years hoping you will not hold that against him.

Following pages: Clooney plays Fred Friendly in *Good Night, and Good Luck* (2005), his own second film.

1961
6 May George Timothy Clooney born to Nicholas Joseph 'Nick' Clooney and Nina Bruce Clooney (née Warren) in Lexington, Kentucky.

1966
17 March Makes television début dressed as a leprechaun on *The Nick Clooney Show*, broadcast in Cincinnati, Ohio.

1974
The Clooney family moves to Augusta, Kentucky, where George will eventually graduate from high school.

1975
Develops Bell's palsy (partial facial paralysis). Recovers after nine months.

1977
Tries out for the Cincinnati Reds professional baseball team. Does not make the cut.

1978
Cast as an extra in NBC TV mini-series *Centennial*, based on a novel by James A. Michener.

1979
Graduates from Augusta High School, and matriculates to Northern Kentucky University with a major in Broadcast Journalism (which he failed to obtain).

1981
Transfers to the University of Cincinnati. Drops out and does various jobs (construction, cutting tobacco, women's shoes salesman) to make ends meet.

1982
Receives extra work in Lexington, Kentucky, on the set of *And They Are Off*, featuring his cousin Miguel Ferrer and uncle José Ferrer.

With encouragement from Miguel (and despite discouragement from Nick), George drives cross-country to Beverly Hills, California, where he moves in with his aunt, the actress and singer Rosemary Clooney.

Takes acting classes at the Beverly Hills Playhouse and begins auditioning for film and television work.

1983
Kicked out of Rosemary Clooney's house. Moves in with a friend, the actor Thom Mathews.

1984
Makes network television début as a kidnapper on NBC action–drama *Riptide*.

Cast as 'Ace' on CBS sitcom *E/R*, opposite Elliott Gould.

1985
Begins two-year stint as series regular on NBC sitcom *The Facts of Life*.

Lands role in as-yet-unreleased *Grizzly II: The Concert* (a.k.a. *Predator: The Concert*).

1987
Appears in low-budget horror parody *Return to Horror High* as Oliver, who does not survive to the end credits.

1988
First starring role as Matt Stevens in *Return of the Killer Tomatoes!*

Cast as series regular on hit ABC sitcom *Roseanne*. Plays Laurie Metcalf's boss and love interest.

1989
Marries Talia Balsam, daughter of actor Martin Balsam.

1991
Written out of *Roseanne*. Books regular gig on series *Baby Talk*, based on the hit movie *Look Who's Talking*.

1992
Baby Talk cancelled.

Plays Mac – the other, younger man – in marital infidelity dramedy *Unbecoming Age* (a.k.a. *The Magic Bubble*).

Books regular role on short-lived CBS cop drama *Bodies of Evidence*.

1993
Divorces Talia Balsam.

Joins cast of NBC drama *Sisters* for one season.

1994
Cast as Dr. Doug Ross on NBC medical drama *ER*. The show immediately becomes the second-highest-rated show on television, and Clooney is its breakout star.

1995
Buys Studio City home previously owned by Clark Gable. Pays cash.

Nominated for first Emmy as Outstanding Lead Actor in a Drama Series for *ER*.

1996
Stars in Robert Rodriguez's *From Dusk Till Dawn* and Michael Hoffman's *One Fine Day*.

Receives first Golden Globe nomination for Best Performance by an Actor in a TV Series (*ER*).

1997
Stars as Batman/Bruce Wayne in *Batman & Robin*. Regrets it for the rest of his life.

Co-stars with Nicole Kidman in *The Peacemaker*, the first feature from DreamWorks SKG.

Named the 'Sexiest Man Alive' by *People Magazine*.

Forms Maysville Pictures at Warner Bros. with veteran producer Robert Lawrence.

1998
Stars in Steven Soderbergh's *Out of Sight*.

Briefly appears in *The Thin Red Line*, Terrence Malick's first film in twenty years.

1999
Leaves *ER* after five seasons.

Stars in David O. Russell's *Three Kings*. On-set fight with Russell leads to a fourteen-year feud.

Closes Maysville Pictures.

2000
Produces and stars in live television broadcast of *Fail Safe*.

Stars in first blockbuster, *The Perfect Storm*.

Stars in *O Brother, Where Art Thou?* Begins long creative relationship with filmmakers Joel and Ethan Coen.

Forms Section Eight Productions at Warner Bros. with Steven Soderbergh.

2001
Section Eight's first release, *Ocean's Eleven*, is a box-office smash.

Wins Golden Globe for Best Performance by an Actor in a Motion Picture – Comedy or Musical (*O Brother, Where Art Thou?*).

2002
Stars in Steven Soderbergh's *Solaris*.

Directorial début: *Confessions of a Dangerous Mind*, a spy comedy with Sam Rockwell and Drew Barrymore.

2003
Co-stars with Catherine Zeta-Jones in the Coen brothers' *Intolerable Cruelty*. Though the film performs modestly at the US box office, it is a hit internationally.

2004
Re-teams with his all-star pals for *Ocean's Twelve*, which does blockbuster business (though slightly less than the first).

2005
Directs and co-writes *Good Night, and Good Luck*. Co-stars as TV producer Fred Friendly.

Puts on thirty-five pounds to

play CIA operative Bob Barnes in Stephen Gaghan's *Syriana*. Injures spinal cord during shoot, thus necessitating years of surgery.

2006
Wins Academy Award for Best Supporting Actor in *Syriana*. Also receives Best Director and Original Screenplay nominations for *Good Night, and Good Luck*.

Amicably agrees with Soderbergh to close down Section Eight. Subsequently forms Smoke House Pictures with Grant Heslov.

Travels to Sudan, thus beginning activism aimed at ending civil war and genocide in the region.

Co-stars with Cate Blanchett in Steven Soderbergh's *The Good German*, which is a critical and commercial disappointment.

2007
Forms Not On Our Watch with Don Cheadle, Matt Damon, Brad Pitt, David Pressman and Jerry Weintraub as a means of raising funds for humanitarian crises.

Stars in Tony Gilroy's *Michael Clayton*.

2008
Receives Academy Award nomination for Best Actor in *Michael Clayton*.

Directs *Leatherheads*.

Joins ensemble cast for the Coen brothers' hit Beltway comedy, *Burn After Reading*.

Named a Messenger of Peace by the United Nations.

2009
Produces and co-stars in Grant Heslov's *The Men Who Stare at Goats*, which fails to catch on with critics and audiences.

Stars as the voice of Mr. Fox in Wes Anderson's stop-motion-animated *Fantastic Mr. Fox*.

Returns for one episode of *ER* in the show's final season.

Stars in Jason Reitman's *Up in the Air*.

Smoke House ends relationship with Warner Bros., moves to Sony Pictures.

2010
Receives Academy Award nomination for Best Actor for *Up in the Air*.

Stars in Anton Corbijn's *The American*.

Launches Satellite Sentinel Project as a means of monitoring war crimes in North and South Sudan.

2011
Directs, co-writes and stars in *The Ides of March*.

Stars in Alexander Payne's *The Descendants*.

2012
Receives Academy Award nomination for Best Actor in *The Descendants*.

Arrested for civil disobedience outside the Sudanese Embassy in Washington, DC. His father, Nick, is also arrested.

2013
Co-stars in Alfonso Cuarón's *Gravity*, opposite Sandra Bullock.

2014
Directs, co-writes and stars in *The Monuments Men*.

27 September Officially weds human rights lawyer Amal Alamuddin at the Ca' Farsetti in Venice, Italy.

2015
Receives Cecil B. DeMille Lifetime Achievement Award

from the Hollywood Foreign Press Association.

Stars in Brad Bird's *Tomorrowland*.

Page 172:
Top, left: Clooney in *From Dusk Till Dawn* (1996) by Robert Rodriguez.

Top, right: Clooney in *The Thin Red Line* (1998) by Terrence Malick.

Bottom, left: Clooney in *The Perfect Storm* (1995) by Wolfgang Petersen.

Bottom, right: Clooney in *Confessions of a Dangerous Mind* (2002) by himself.

Opposite:
Top, left: Clooney in *Intolerable Cruelty* (2003) by Joel Coen.

Top, right: Clooney in *Ocean's Twelve* (2004) by Steven Soderbergh.

Bottom, left: Clooney in *Leatherheads* (2008) by himself.

Bottom, right: Clooney in *The Ides of March* (2011) by himself.

Page 176:
Top, left: Poster for *From Dusk Till Dawn* (1996) by Robert Rodriguez.

Top, right: Poster for *Syriana* (2005) by Stephen Gaghan.

Bottom, left: Poster for *The American* (2010) by Anton Corbijn.

Bottom, right: Poster for *Gravity* (2013) by Alfonso Cuarón.

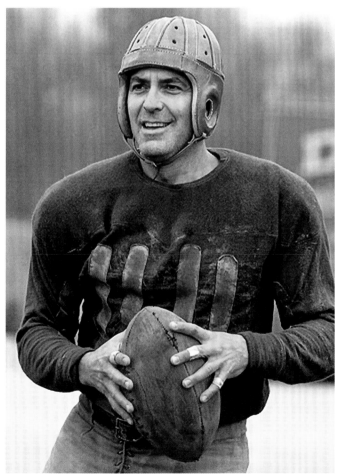

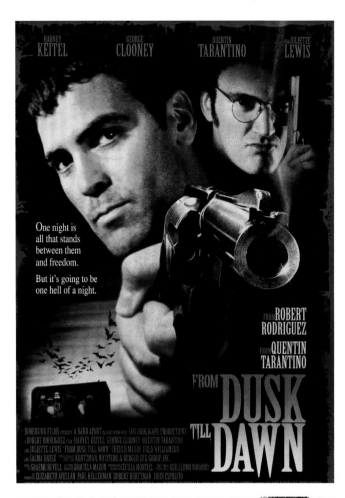

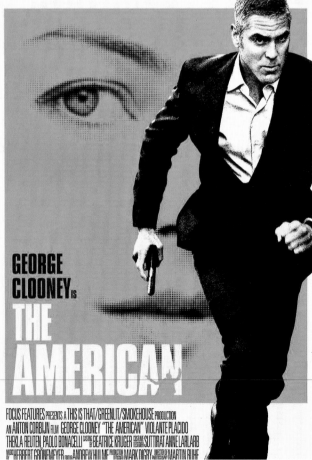

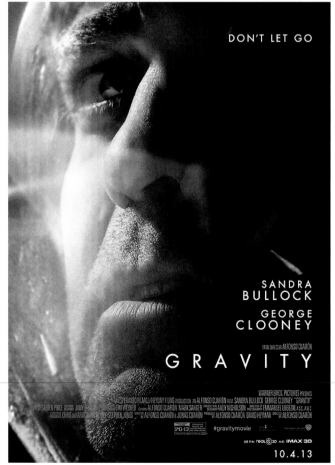

1978
Centennial (TV mini-series)
Creator John Wilder, from a novel by James A. Michener. With George Clooney (Village Extra, uncredited), Richard Chamberlain (Alexander McKeag), Michael Ansara (Lame Beaver), Robert Conrad (Pasquinel), Raymond Burr (Herman Bockweiss), Lynn Redgrave (Charlotte Buckland Seccombe), Andy Griffith (Professor Lewis Vernor), Merle Haggard (Cisco Calendar), Brian Keith (Sheriff Axel Dumire).

1982
And They Are Off (unreleased film)
Director Theodore H. Kuhns III *Screenwriter* A. Theodore Kuhns II *Director of Photography* Paul Lohmann *Composer* Bill Conti *Film Editor* Richard G. Haines *Producer* A. Theodore Kuhns II. With George Clooney (extra), José Ferrer (Martin Craig), Tab Hunter (Henry Barclay), Juanita Moore (Sadie Johnson), Adam Roarke (Dale Campbell).

1984
Riptide (TV series)
'Where the Girls Are' (Season 2, Episode 1, 2 October 1984)
Creators Stephen J. Cannell and Frank Lupo *Director* Ron Satlof *Screenwriter* Babs Greyhosky *Composers* Mike Post and Pete Carpenter *Producer* Tom Blomquist. With George Clooney (Lenny Colwell), Perry King (Cody

Allen), Joe Penny (Nick Ryder), Thom Bray (Murray 'Boz' Bozinsky).

1984–5
E/R (TV series)
'Both Sides Now' (Season 1, Episode 14, 12 December 1984)
'The Storm' (Season 1, Episode 15, 19 December 1984)
'Enter Romance' (Season 1, Episode 16, 26 December 1984)
'Brotherly Love' (Season 1, Episode 17, 16 January 1985)
'I Raise You' (Season 1, Episode 18, 23 January 1985)
'Merry Wives of Sheinfeld: Part 1' (Season 1, Episode 19, 30 January 1985)
'Merry Wives of Sheinfeld: Part 2' (Season 1, Episode 20, 6 February 1985)
'A Change in Policy' (Season 1, Episode 22, 27 February 1985)
Creator The Organic Theater Company and Dr. Ronald Berman *Director* Peter Bonerz *Composer* Jimmy Webb *Producer* Eve Brandstein. With George Clooney (Mark 'Ace' Kolmar), Elliott Gould (Dr. Howard Sheinfeld), Mary McDonnell (Dr. Eve Sheridan), Conchata Ferrell (Nurse Joan Thor), Lynne Moody (Nurse Julie Williams), Shuko Akune (Maria Amardo), Bruce A. Young (Officer Fred Burdock).

1985
Street Hawk (TV series)
'A Second Self' (Season 1, Episode 2, 11 January 1985)

Creators Paul M. Belous, Bruce Lansbury and Robert Wolterstorff *Director* Virgil W. Vogel *Screenwriters* Bruce Cervi and Nicholas Corea *Director of Photography* Frank P. Flynn *Composer* Tangerine Dream *Film Editor* Neil MacDonald *Producers* Burton Armus, Stephen Cragg and Karen Harris. With George Clooney (Kevin Stark), Rex Smith (Jesse Mach), Joe Regalbuto (Norman Tuttle), Richard Venture (Lt. Cmdr. Leo Altobelli), Jeannie Wilson (Rachel Adams).

Crazy Like a Fox (TV series)
'Suitable for Framing' (Season 1, Episode 12, 31 March 1985)
Creators Roger Shulman, John Baskin, George Schenck and Frank Cardea *Director* Paul Krasny *Screenwriter* Tim Maschler. With George Clooney (unnamed character), Jack Warden (Harrison 'Harry' Fox, Sr), John Rubinstein (Harrison Fox), Penny Peyser (Cindy Fox), Robby Kiger (Josh Fox).

Grizzly II: The Concert (unreleased film)
Director André Szöts *Screenwriters* Joan McCall and David Sheldon *Director of Photography* László Kovács *Film Editor* Paris Éclair Lab *Producers* Ross Massbaum, Suzanne Nagy, Joseph Ford Proctor and David Sheldon. With George Clooney (mountain man), Steve Inwood (Nick Hollister), Deborah Raffin (Samantha Owens), John

Rhys-Davies (Bouchard), Louise Fletcher (Eileene Draygon), Deborah Foreman (Chrissy Hollister).

1985–7
The Facts of Life (TV series)
17 Episodes (from Seasons 7 and 8)
Creators Dick Clair, Jenna McMahon, Howard Leeds, Jerry Mayer and Ben Starr *Composer* Ray Colcord. With George Clooney (George Burnett), Charlotte Rae (Edna Garrett), Lisa Whelchel (Blair Warner), Kim Fields (Dorothy 'Tootie' Ramsey), Mindy Cohn (Natalie Green), Nancy McKeon (Jo Polniaczek).

1986
Hotel (TV series)
'Recriminations' (Season 3, Episode 13, 29 January 1986)
Creators John Furia and Barry Oringer *Director* Nancy Malone *Screenwriters* Mitch Paradise and Arlene Stadd, from her story and a novel by Arthur Hailey *Director of Photography* Robert C. Moreno *Set Decorator* Joseph A. Armetta *Composer* Angela Morley *Film Editor* Barry L. Gold *Producers* Henry Colman and Geoffrey Fischer. With George Clooney (Nick Miller), Anne Baxter (Victoria Cabot), James Brolin (Peter McDermott), Connie Sellecca (Christine Francis), Shea Farrell (Mark Danning).

Throb (TV series)
'My Fair Punker Lady' (Season 1, Episode 4, 11 October 1986)

Creator Fredi Towbin
Director Linda Day
Screenwriter Hollis Rich,
from a story by Sandy
Krinski *Composer* The
Nylons *Producer* Fredi
Towbin. With George
Clooney (Rollo Moldonado),
Diana Canova (Sandy
Beatty), Jonathan Prince
(Zachary Armstrong),
Maryedith Burrell
(Meredith), Jane Leeves
(Prudence Anne 'Blue'
Bartlett).

Combat High (TV movie)
Director Neal Israel
Screenwriter Paul W. Shapiro
Director of Photography
Steve Yaconelli *Composer*
Robert Folk *Set Decorator*
Roy Alan Amaral *Film
Editors* Tom Finan and
Mike Hill *Producer*
Robert M. Sertner. With
George Clooney (Cadet
Major Biff Woods), Keith
Gordon (Max Mendelsson),
Wallace Langham (Perry
Barnett), Dana Hill (Cadet
Sergeant Andrea Pritchett),
Tina Caspary (Mary Beth),
Robert Culp (General
Edward 'Ed' Woods),
Sherman Hemsley (Judge
Daley).

1987
Return to Horror High
Director Bill Froehlich
Screenwriters Bill Froehlich,
Mark Lisson, Dana
Escalante and Greg H. Sims
Director of Photography
Roy H. Wagner *Composer*
Stacy Widelitz *Film Editor*
Nancy Forner *Producer*
Mark Lisson. With George
Clooney (Oliver), Lori
Lethin (Callie Cassidy/Sarah
Walker/Susan), Brendan
Hughes (Steven Blake),
Alex Rocco (Harry Sleerik),
Scott Jacoby (Josh Forbes),
Andy Romano (Principal
Kastleman), Maureen
McCormick (Officer Tyler),
Vince Edwards (Richard
Birnbaum).

Hunter (TV series)
'Double Exposure'
(Season 3, Episode 15,
14 February 1987)
Creator Frank Lupo *Director*
James Whitmore, Jr
Screenwriters Thomas and
Charlotte Huggins *Director
of Photography* Roland
'Ozzie' Smith *Set Decorator*
W. Joe Kroesser *Composers*
Pete Carpenter and Mike Post
Film Editor John Elias
Producers David G. Phinney
and Stu Segall. With George
Clooney (Matthew Winfield),
Fred Dryer (Detective
Sergeant Rick Hunter),
Stepfanie Kramer (Detective
Sergeant Dee Dee McCall),
Charles Hallahan (Captain
Charles Devane), Garrett
Morris (Sporty James).

Murder, She Wrote (TV series)
'No Laughing Murder'
(Season 3, Episode 18,
15 March 1987)
Creators Peter S. Fischer,
Richard Levinson and
William Link *Director* Walter
Grauman *Screenwriter*
Tom Sawyer *Director
of Photography* Robert C.
Moreno *Set Decorator* Robert
Wingo *Composer* Richard
Markowitz *Film Editor*
Donald Douglas *Producer*
Robert F. O'Neill. With
George Clooney (Kip
Howard), Angela Lansbury
(Jessica Fletcher), Beth
Windsor (Corrie Gruen),
Buddy Hackett (Murray
Gruen), Steve Lawrence
(Mack Howard).

The Golden Girls (TV series)
'To Catch a Neighbor'
(Season 2, Episode 24,
2 May 1987)
Creator Susan Harris
Director Terry Hughes
Screenwriter Russell Marcus
Composer George Aliceson
Tipton *Film Editor* Harold
McKenzie *Producers* Terry
Grossman and Kathy Speer.
With George Clooney
(Bobby Hopkins), Bea
Arthur (Dorothy Zbornak),
Betty White (Rose Nylund),

Rue McClanahan (Blanche
Devereaux), Estelle Getty
(Sophia Petrillo).

Bennett Brothers (TV movie)
Director Will Mackenzie
Screenwriter Lloyd Garver
Composer David Frishberg
Producer Bettina Bennewitz.
With George Clooney
(Tom Bennett), Richard
Kind (Richard Bennett),
Alan North (Manny Bennett),
Peggy Pope (Shirley Bennett).

1988
Return of the Killer Tomatoes!
Director John De Bello
Screenwriters Stephen F.
Andrich, John De Bello, Costa
Dillon and J. Stephen Peace
Directors of Photography
Victor Lou and Stephen Welch
Set Decorator Melinda Ritz
Composers Neal Fox and
Rick Patterson *Film Editors*
Stephen F. Andrich and John
De Bello *Producer* J. Stephen
Peace. With George Clooney
(Matt Stevens), Anthony
Starke (Chad Finletter),
Karen M. Waldron (Tara
Boumdeay), Steve Lundquist
(Igor), John Astin (Professor
Gangreen).

1988–91
Roseanne (TV series)
'Life and Stuff' (Season 1,
Episode 1, 18 October 1988)
'Radio Days'
(Season 1, Episode 5,
29 November 1988)
'Lovers' Lane' (Season 1,
Episode 6, 6 December 1988)
'The Memory Game'
(Season 1, Episode 7,
13 December 1988)
'Here's to Good Friends'
(Season 1, Episode 8,
20 December 1988)
'Dan's Birthday Bash'
(Season 1, Episode 9,
3 January 1989)
'Canoga Time' (Season 1,
Episode 11, 17 January 1989)
'Bridge Over Troubled
Sonny' (Season 1,
Episode 13, 31 January 1989)
'Workin' Overtime'
(Season 1, Episode 19,
14 March 1989)

'Let's Call It Quits'
(Season 1, Episode 23,
2 May 1989)
'Trick Me Up, Trick Me Down'
(Season 4, Episode 6,
29 October 1991)
Creator Matt Williams
Director of Photography
Daniel Flannery *Composers*
Dan Foliart and Howard
Pearl. With George Clooney
(Booker Brooks), Roseanne
Barr (Roseanne Conner),
John Goodman (Dan
Conner), Laurie Metcalf
(Jackie Harris), Sara Gilbert
(Darlene Conner), Michael
Fishman (D.J. Conner), Alicia
Goranson (Becky Conner).

1989
Red Surf (video)
Director H. Gordon Boos
Screenwriter Vincent Robert,
from a story by Jason Hoffs,
Brian Gamble and Vincent
Robert *Director of
Photography* John
Schwartzman *Composer*
Sasha Matson *Film Editor*
Dennis Dolan *Producer*
Richard Weinman. With
George Clooney (Remar),
Doug Savant (Attila),
Dedee Pfeiffer (Rebecca),
Philip McKeon (True Blue).

1990
Knights of the Kitchen Table
(TV movie)
With George Clooney (Rick
Stepjack), Jessica Steen (Marla
McDermott), Andrew Lauer
(Lewis), Rick Aiello (Barry).

Sunset Beat (TV movie, pilot
for the eponymous series)
Directors Bill Corcoran and
Sam Weisman *Director of
Photography* Peter Stein
Composer Peter Bernstein
Producer Justis Greene.
With George Clooney (Chic
Chesbro), Michael DeLuise
(Tim Kelly), Markus Flanagan
(Bradley Coolidge).

1990–2
Sunset Beat (TV series)
'One Down, Four Up'
(Season 1, Episode 1,
21 April 1990)

'Rebel Dreams'
(Season 1, Episode 3,
25 November 1992)
With George Clooney
(Chic Chesbro), Jason Stuart
(Marty), Michael DeLuise
(Tim Kelly).

1991
Baby Talk (TV series)
'Baby Love' (Season 1,
Episode 1, 8 March 1991)
'A Star Is Newborn'
(Season 1, Episode 2,
15 March 1991)
'Womb with a View'
(Season 1, Episode 3,
22 March 1991)
'Trading Places' (Season 1,
Episode 4, 29 March 1991)
'Out of Africa' (Season 1,
Episode 12, 17 May 1991)
Creator Ed. Weinberger,
from characters created
by Amy Heckerling *Director*
John Bowab *Director of
Photography* Daniel Flannery
Composer Bill Maxwell
Film Editor Charlie Bowyer
Producers Dennis Gallegos,
Mark J. Greenberg, Maxine
Lapiduss and Patricia Fass
Palmer. With George Clooney
(Joe), Julia Duffy (Maggie
Campbell), Ryan and Paul
Jessup (Mickey Campbell),
Lenny Wolpe (Howard),
William Hickey (Mr. Fogarty),
Tom Alan Robbins (Dr. Elliot
Fleisher), Tony Danza (voice
of Mickey Campbell).

Rewrite for Murder
(TV movie)
Director Eric Laneuville
Screenwriter Michael Gleason
Director of Photography
Dennis Matsuda *Composer*
Tom Scott *Set Decorator*
W. Joe Kroesser *Film Editors*
Steve Polivka and Randy
Roberts *Producer* Gareth
Davies. With George Clooney,
Pam Dawber, Greg Germann,
Patrick Bristow, Dennis
Lipscomb.

1992
Unbecoming Age
Directors Alfredo and
Deborah Ringel *Screenwriters*
Meridith Baer and Geof

Prysirr *Director of
Photography* Harry Mathias
Set Decorator Daryn-Reid
Goodall *Composer* Jeff Lass
Film Editor Alan James
Geik *Producers* Alfredo
and Deborah Ringel. With
George Clooney (Mac), Diane
Salinger (Julia), John Calvin
(Charles), Colleen Camp
(Deborah), Priscilla Pointer
(Grandma).

Jack's Place (TV series)
'Everything Old Is New
Again' (Season 1, Episode 4,
23 June 1992)
Director Charles Siebert
Composers Bill Elliott and
David Schwartz *Film Editor*
Augie Hess. With George
Clooney (Rick Logan),
Denise Crosby (Lindsay),
John Dye (Greg Toback),
Michele Greene (Suzanne),
Finola Hughes (Chelsea
Duffy), Hal Linden (Jack
Evans), Courtney Thorne-
Smith (Kim Logan).

The Harvest
Director David Marconi
Screenwriter David Marconi
Director of Photography
Emmanuel Lubezki *Set
Decorator* Graciela Torres
Composer Rick Boston
Film Editor Carlos Puente
Producers Jason Clark
and Morgan Mason. With
George Clooney (Lip Syncing
Transvestite), Miguel Ferrer
(Charlie Pope), Leilani Sarelle
(Natalie Caldwell), Henry
Silva (Detective Topo), Tony
Denison (Noel Guzmann),
Tim Thomerson (Steve
Mobley), Harvey Fierstein
(Bob Lakin).

1992–3
Bodies of Evidence
(TV series)
16 Episodes (Season 1,
Episode 1–Season 2,
Episode 8)
Creators James L. Conway
and David Jacobs *Composer*
Christopher Klatman
Producer Joel J. Feigenbaum.
With George Clooney
(Detective Ryan Walker),

Lee Horsley (Lieutenant
Ben Carroll), Kate McNeil
(Detective Nora Houghton),
Al Fann (Detective Will
Stratton), Leslie Jordan
(Lemar Samuels).

1993
*Without Warning: Terror
in the Towers* (TV movie)
Director Alan J. Levi
Screenwriters Stephen
Downing and Duane Poole
Director of Photography
Chuy Elizondo *Composer*
Jay Gruska *Set Decorator*
Sean Kennedy *Film Editors*
Kate McGowan and
M. Edward Salier *Producers*
Stephen Downing and
Robert M. Rolsky. With
George Clooney (Kevin Shea),
James Avery (Fred Ferby),
Fran Drescher (Rosemarie
Russo), John Karlen (Jack
McAllister), Scott Plank
(Gary Geidel).

The Building (TV Series)
Pilot Episode (20 August
1993)
Creator Bonnie Hunt
Director of Photography
Jo Mayer *Producers* John
Bowab, Dan Jackson and
Robert Wright. With George
Clooney (Bonnie's Fiancé),
Bonnie Hunt (Bonnie
Kennedy), Mike Hagerty
(Finley), Richard Kuhlman
(Big Tony), Don Lake (Brad),
Tom Virtue (Stanley), Holly
Wortell (Holly).

1993–4
Sisters (TV series)
19 Episodes (Season 4,
Episode 2–Season 5,
Episode 3)
Creators Ron Cowen and
Daniel Lipman. With George
Clooney (Detective James
Falconer), Swoosie Kurtz
(Alex Reed), Patricia
Kalember (Georgie Reed
Whitsig), Sela Ward (Teddy
Reed Margolis), Julianne
Phillips (Francesca 'Frankie'
Reed Margolis).

1994–2009
ER (TV series)
109 Episodes (Seasons 1–4;
Season 5, Episodes 1–15;
Season 6, Episode 21;
Season 15, Episode 19)
Creator Michael Crichton
Composer Martin Davich
Producers Michael Crichton
and John Wells. With George
Clooney (Dr. Doug Ross),
Laura Innes (Dr. Kerry
Weaver), Noah Wyle
(Dr. John Carter), Sherry
Stringfield (Dr. Susan Lewis),
Eriq La Salle (Dr. Peter
Benton), Anthony Edwards
(Dr. Mark Greene), Julianna
Margulies (Nurse Carol
Hathaway), Gloria Reuben
(Jeanie Boulet), Ellen
Crawford (Nurse Lydia
Wright), Lily Mariye (Nurse
Lily Jarvik), Deezer D (Nurse
Malik McGrath).

1995
Friends (TV series)
'The One With Two Parts'
(Season 1, Episodes 16
and 17, 23 February 1995)
Creators David Crane and
Marta Kauffman *Director*
Michael Lembeck
Screenwriters David Crane
and Marta Kauffman
Director of Photography
Richard Hissong *Set
Decorator* Greg J. Grande
Film Editor Andy Zall
Producer Todd Stevens. With
George Clooney (Dr. Michael
Mitchell), Jennifer Aniston
(Rachel Green), Courteney
Cox (Monica Geller), Lisa
Kudrow (Phoebe Buffay/
Ursula Buffay), Matt LeBlanc
(Joey Tribbiani), Matthew
Perry (Chandler Bing), David
Schwimmer (Dr. Ross Geller),
Noah Wyle (Dr. Jeffrey
Rosen).

1996
From Dusk Till Dawn
Director Robert Rodriguez
Screenwriter Quentin
Tarantino, from a story by
Robert Kurtzman *Director
of Photography* Guillermo
Navarro *Set Decorator* Felipe
Fernández del Paso *Composer*

Graeme Revell *Film Editor* Robert Rodriguez *Producers* Gianni Nunnari and Meir Teper. With George Clooney (Seth Gecko), Quentin Tarantino (Richard Gecko), Harvey Keitel (Jacob Fuller), Juliette Lewis (Kate Fuller), Ernest Liu (Scott Fuller), Salma Hayek (Santanico Pandemonium).

One Fine Day
Director Michael Hoffman *Screenwriters* Terrel Seltzer and Ellen Simon *Director of Photography* Oliver Stapleton *Set Decorator* Anne Kuljian *Composer* James Newton Howard *Film Editor* Garth Craven *Producer* Lynda Obst. With George Clooney (Jack Taylor), Michelle Pfeiffer (Melanie Parker), Mae Whitman (Maggie Taylor), Alex D. Linz (Sammy Parker), Charles Durning (Lew).

1997
Batman & Robin
Director Joel Schumacher *Screenwriter* Akiva Goldsman, from characters created by Bob Kane *Director of Photography* Stephen Goldblatt *Set Decorator* Dorree Cooper *Composer* Elliot Goldenthal *Film Editors* Mark Stevens and Dennis Virkler *Producer* Peter MacGregor-Scott. With George Clooney (Batman/Bruce Wayne), Arnold Schwarzenegger (Mr. Freeze/Dr. Victor Fries), Chris O'Donnell (Robin/Dick Grayson), Uma Thurman (Poison Ivy/Dr. Pamela Isley), Alicia Silverstone (Batgirl/Barbara Wilson).

South Park (TV series)
'Big Gay Al's Big Gay Boat Ride' (Season 1, Episode 4, 3 September 1997)
Creators Trey Parker, Matt Stone and Brian Graden *Screenwriters* Matt Stone and Trey Parker *Composer* Adam Berry *Film Editor* John Laus *Producer* Anne Garefino. With the voices of George

Clooney (Sparky the Dog), Trey Parker (numerous), Matt Stone (numerous), Mary Kay Bergman (numerous), Isaac Hayes (Chef).

The Peacemaker
Director Mimi Leder *Screenwriter* Michael Schiffer, from an article by Leslie and Andrew Cockburn *Director of Photography* Dietrich Lohmann *Set Decorator* Rosemary Brandenburg *Composer* Hans Zimmer *Film Editor* David Rosenbloom *Producers* Branko Lustig and Walter F. Parkes. With George Clooney (Lt. Col. Thomas Devoe), Nicole Kidman (Dr. Julia Kelly), Marcel Iures (Dusan Gavrich), Aleksandr Baluev (General Aleksandr Kodoroff), Armin Mueller-Stahl (Dimitri Vertikoff).

1998
Murphy Brown (TV series)
'Never Can Say Goodbye: Part 2' (Season 10, Episode 22, 18 May 1998)
Creator Diane English *Director* Barnet Kellman *Screenwriter* Diane English *Director of Photography* Gil Hubbs *Composer* Steve Dorff *Film Editor* Tucker Wiard *Producer* Bob Jeffords. With George Clooney (Doctor #2), Candice Bergen (Murphy Brown), Faith Ford (Corky Sherwood), Joe Regalbuto (Frank Fontana), Charles Kimbrough (Jim Dial), Lily Tomlin (Kay Carter-Shepley).

Out of Sight
Director Steven Soderbergh *Screenwriter* Scott Frank, from a novel by Elmore Leonard *Director of Photography* Elliot Davis *Set Decorator* Maggie Martin *Composer* David Holmes *Film Editor* Anne V. Coates *Producers* Danny DeVito, Michael Shamberg and Stacey Sher. With George Clooney (Jack Foley), Jennifer Lopez (Karen Sisco), Ving Rhames (Buddy Bragg), Don Cheadle

(Maurice Miller), Catherine Keener (Adele), Dennis Farina (Marshall Sisco), Albert Brooks (Richard Ripley).

The Thin Red Line
Director Terrence Malick *Screenwriter* Terrence Malick, from a novel by James Jones *Director of Photography* John Toll *Set Decorators* Richard Hobbs and Suza Maybury *Composer* Hans Zimmer *Film Editors* Leslie Jones, Saar Klein and Billy Weber *Producers* Robert Michael Geisler, Grant Hill and John Roberdeau. With George Clooney (Captain Charles Bosche), Sean Penn (1st Sergeant Edward Welsh), Adrien Brody (Corporal Fife), Jim Caviezel (Private Witt), Ben Chaplin (Private Bell), John Cusack (Captain John Gaff), Nick Nolte (Lt. Col. Gordon Tall), Elias Koteas (Captain James 'Bugger' Staros), John C. Reilly (Sergeant Storm), Woody Harrelson (Sergeant Keck).

1999
South Park: Bigger, Longer & Uncut
Director Trey Parker *Screenwriters* Trey Parker, Matt Stone and Pam Brady, from the television series *South Park* by Trey Parker and Matt Stone *Composer* Marc Shaiman *Film Editor* John Venzon *Producers* Trey Parker and Matt Stone. With the voices of George Clooney (Dr. Gouache), Trey Parker (numerous), Matt Stone (numerous), Mary Kay Bergman (numerous), Isaac Hayes (Chef).

Three Kings
Director David O. Russell *Screenwriter* David O. Russell, from a story by John Ridley *Director of Photography* Newton Thomas Sigel *Set Decorator* Gene Serdena *Composer* Carter Burwell *Film Editor* Robert K. Lambert *Producers* Paul Junger Witt, Charles

Roven and Edward McDonnell. With George Clooney (Archie Gates), Mark Wahlberg (Troy Barlow), Ice Cube (Chief Elgin), Spike Jonze (Conrad Vig), Cliff Curtis (Amir Abdulah), Nora Dunn (Adriana Cruz).

2000
Fail Safe (TV movie)
Director Stephen Frears *Screenwriter* Walter Bernstein, from a novel by Eugene Burdick and Harvey Wheeler *Director of Photography* John A. Alonzo *Set Decorator* Alice Baker *Producer* Tom Park. With George Clooney (Colonel Jack Grady), Richard Dreyfuss (The President), Noah Wyle (Buck), Brian Dennehy (General Bogan), Sam Elliott (Congressman Raskob), James Cromwell (Gordon Knapp), John Diehl (Colonel Cascio), Hank Azaria (Professor Groeteschele), Norman Lloyd (Defense Secretary Swenson), Don Cheadle (Lieutenant Jimmy Pierce), Harvey Keitel (Brig. Gen. Warren Black).

The Perfect Storm
Director Wolfgang Petersen *Screenwriter* William D. Wittliff, from a book by Sebastian Junger *Director of Photography* John Seale *Set Decorator* Ernie Bishop *Composer* James Horner *Film Editor* Richard Francis-Bruce *Producers* Gail Katz, Wolfgang Petersen and Paula Weinstein. With George Clooney (Captain Billy Tyne), Mark Wahlberg (Bobby Shatford), Diane Lane (Christina Cotter), John C. Reilly (Dale 'Murph' Murphy), William Fichtner (David 'Sully' Sullivan).

O Brother, Where Art Thou?
Director Joel Coen *Screenwriters* Joel and Ethan Coen, from an epic poem by Homer *Director of Photography* Roger Deakins *Set Decorator* Nancy Haigh

Composer T Bone Burnett *Film Editors* Joel and Ethan Coen (as Roderick Jaynes) and Tricia Cooke *Producer* Ethan Coen. With George Clooney (Everett), John Turturro (Pete Hogwallop), Tim Blake Nelson (Delmar O'Donnell), John Goodman (Big Dan Teague), Holly Hunter (Penny), Chris Thomas King (Tommy Johnson), Charles Durning (Pappy O'Daniel).

2001
Spy Kids
Director Robert Rodriguez *Screenwriter* Robert Rodriguez *Director of Photography* Guillermo Navarro *Set Decorator* Jeanette Scott *Composers* John Debney, Danny Elfman, Los Lobos and Robert Rodriguez *Film Editor* Robert Rodriguez *Producers* Elizabeth Avellan and Robert Rodriguez. With George Clooney (Devlin), Alexa PenaVega (Carmen Cortez), Daryl Sabara (Juni Cortez), Antonio Banderas (Gregorio Cortez), Carla Gugino (Ingrid Cortez), Alan Cumming (Fegan Floop), Tony Shalhoub (Alexander Minion), Teri Hatcher (Ms. Gradenko).

Ocean's Eleven
Director Steven Soderbergh *Screenwriter* Ted Griffin, from a screenplay (1960) by Harry Brown and Charles Lederer and on a story by George Clayton Johnson and Jack Golden Russell *Director of Photography* Steven Soderbergh (as Peter Andrews) *Set Decorator* Kristen Toscano Messina *Composer* David Holmes *Film Editor* Stephen Mirrione *Producer* Jerry Weintraub. With George Clooney (Danny Ocean), Matt Damon (Linus Caldwell), Andy Garcia (Terry Benedict), Brad Pitt (Rusty Ryan), Julia Roberts (Tess Ocean), Don Cheadle (Basher Tarr), Bernie Mac (Frank Catton), Elliott Gould

(Reuben Tishkoff), Casey Affleck (Virgil Malloy), Scott Caan (Turk Malloy), Shaobo Qin (Yen), Eddie Jemison (Livingston Dell), Carl Reiner (Saul Bloom).

2002
Welcome to Collinwood
Directors Anthony and Joe Russo *Screenwriters* Anthony and Joe Russo *Directors of Photography* Charles Minsky and Lisa Rinzler *Set Decorator* Meg Everist *Composer* Mark Mothersbaugh *Film Editor* Amy E. Duddleston *Producers* George Clooney and Steven Soderbergh. With George Clooney (Jerzy), William H. Macy (Riley), Isaiah Washington (Leon), Sam Rockwell (Pero), Michael Jeter (Toto), Luis Guzmán (Cosimo), Patricia Clarkson (Rosalind).

Solaris
Director Steven Soderbergh *Screenwriter* Steven Soderbergh, from a novel by Stanisław Lem *Director of Photography* Steven Soderbergh (as Peter Andrews) *Set Decorators* Mike Malone and Kristen Toscano Messina *Composer* Cliff Martinez *Film Editor* Steven Soderbergh (as Mary Ann Bernard) *Producers* James Cameron and Rae Sanchini. With George Clooney (Chris Kelvin), Natascha McElhone (Rheya), Viola Davis (Gordon), Jeremy Davies (Snow), Ulrich Tukur (Gibarian).

Confessions of a Dangerous Mind
Director George Clooney *Screenwriter* Charlie Kaufman, from a book by Chuck Barris *Director of Photography* Newton Thomas Sigel *Set Decorators* Louis Dandonneau, Anne Galéa and Robert Greenfield *Composer* Alex Wurman *Film Editor* Stephen Mirrione *Producer* Andrew Lazar. With

George Clooney (Jim Byrd), Drew Barrymore (Penny), Julia Roberts (Patricia Watson), Sam Rockwell (Chuck Barris), Maggie Gyllenhaal (Debbie), Rutger Hauer (Keeler).

2003
Spy Kids 3-D: Game Over
Director Robert Rodriguez *Screenwriter* Robert Rodriguez *Director of Photography* Robert Rodriguez *Set Decorators* David Hack and Jeanette Scott *Composers* Robert and Rebecca Rodriguez *Film Editor* Robert Rodriguez *Producers* Elizabeth Avellan and Robert Rodriguez. With George Clooney (Devlin), Alexa PenaVega (Carmen Cortez), Daryl Sabara (Juni Cortez), Antonio Banderas (Gregorio Cortez), Carla Gugino (Ingrid Cortez), Sylvester Stallone (Toymaker), Ricardo Montalban (Grandfather).

Intolerable Cruelty
Director Joel Coen *Screenwriters* Robert Ramsey, Matthew Stone, Ethan and Joel Coen, from a story by Robert Ramsey, Matthew Stone and John Romano *Director of Photography* Roger Deakins *Set Decorator* Nancy Haigh *Composer* Carter Burwell *Film Editors* Ethan and Joel Coen (as Roderick Jaynes) *Producers* Ethan Coen and Brian Grazer. With George Clooney (Miles Massey), Catherine Zeta-Jones (Marylin Hamilton Rexroth Doyle Massey), Geoffrey Rush (Donovan Donaly), Cedric the Entertainer (Gus Petch), Edward Herrmann (Rex Rexroth).

2004
Ocean's Twelve
Director Steven Soderbergh *Screenwriter* George Nolfi, from characters created by George Clayton Johnson and Jack Golden Russell *Director of Photography*

Steven Soderbergh (as Peter Andrews) *Set Decorator* Kristen Toscano Messina *Composer* David Holmes *Film Editor* Stephen Mirrione *Producer* Jerry Weintraub. With George Clooney (Danny Ocean), Brad Pitt (Rusty Ryan), Matt Damon (Linus Caldwell), Catherine Zeta-Jones (Isabel Lahiri), Andy Garcia (Terry Benedict), Don Cheadle (Basher Tarr), Bernie Mac (Frank Catton), Julia Roberts (Tess Ocean).

2005
Good Night, and Good Luck
Director George Clooney *Screenwriters* George Clooney and Grant Heslov *Director of Photography* Robert Elswit *Set Decorator* Jan Pascale *Composer* Jim Papoulis *Film Editor* Stephen Mirrione *Producer* Grant Heslov. With George Clooney (Fred Friendly), David Strathairn (Edward R. Murrow), Frank Langella (William Paley), Patricia Clarkson (Shirley Wershba), Robert Downey, Jr (Joe Wershba), Jeff Daniels (Sig Mickelson).

Syriana
Director Stephen Gaghan *Screenwriter* Stephen Gaghan, from a book by Robert Baer *Director of Photography* Robert Elswit *Set Decorators* Jan Pascale and Olivia Bloch-Lainé *Composer* Alexandre Desplat *Film Editor* Tim Squyres *Producers* Jennifer Fox, Georgia Kacandes and Michael Nozik. With George Clooney (Bob Barnes), Matt Damon (Bryan Woodman), Jeffrey Wright (Bennett Holiday), Chris Cooper (Jimmy Pope), William Hurt (Stan), Kayvan Novak (Arash), Christopher Plummer (Dean Whiting), Amanda Peet (Julie Woodman), Mazhar Munir (Wasim Khan), Alexander Siddig (Prince Nasir Al-Subaai), Mark Strong (Mussawi).

2006
The Good German
Director Steven Soderbergh *Screenwriter* Paul Attanasio, from a novel by Joseph Kanon *Director of Photography* Steven Soderbergh (as Peter Andrews) *Set Decorator* Kristen Toscano Messina *Composer* Thomas Newman *Film Editor* Steven Soderbergh (as Mary Ann Bernard) *Producers* Ben Cosgrove and Gregory Jacobs. With George Clooney (Jake Geismar), Cate Blanchett (Lena Brandt), Tobey Maguire (Tully), Beau Bridges (Colonel Muller), Tony Curran (Danny), Robin Weigert (Hannelore).

2007
Ocean's Thirteen
Director Steven Soderbergh *Screenwriters* Brian Koppelman and David Levien, from characters created by George Clayton Johnson and Jack Golden Russell *Director of Photography* Steven Soderbergh (as Peter Andrews) *Set Decorator* Kristen Toscano Messina *Composer* David Holmes *Film Editor* Stephen Mirrione *Producer* Jerry Weintraub. With George Clooney (Danny Ocean), Brad Pitt (Rusty Ryan), Matt Damon (Linus Caldwell/Lenny Pepperidge), Andy Garcia (Terry Benedict), Don Cheadle (Basher Tarr/Fender Roads), Bernie Mac (Frank Catton), Ellen Barkin (Abigail Sponder), Al Pacino (Willy Bank).

Michael Clayton
Director Tony Gilroy *Screenwriter* Tony Gilroy *Director of Photography* Robert Elswit *Set Decorators* Paul Cheponis, George DeTitta, Jr, Christine Mayer and Chuck Potter *Composer* James Newton Howard *Film Editor* John Gilroy *Producers* Jennifer Fox, Kerry Orent, Sydney Pollack and Steve Samuels. With George Clooney (Michael Clayton), Tilda Swinton (Karen Crowder), Tom Wilkinson (Arthur Edens), Sydney Pollack (Marty Bach), Merritt Wever (Anna).

2008
Leatherheads
Director George Clooney *Screenwriters* Duncan Brantley and Rick Reilly *Director of Photography* Newton Thomas Sigel *Set Decorator* Jan Pascale *Composer* Randy Newman *Film Editor* Stephen Mirrione *Producers* Grant Heslov and Casey Silver. With George Clooney (Dodge Connelly), John Krasinski (Carter Rutherford), Renée Zellweger (Lexie Littleton), Jonathan Pryce (CC Frazier).

Burn After Reading
Directors Joel and Ethan Coen *Screenwriters* Joel and Ethan Coen *Director of Photography* Emmanuel Lubezki *Set Decorator* Nancy Haigh *Composer* Carter Burwell *Film Editors* Joel and Ethan Coen (as Roderick Jaynes) *Producers* Joel and Ethan Coen. With George Clooney (Harry Pfarrer), Frances McDormand (Linda Litzke), Tilda Swinton (Katie Cox), John Malkovich (Osborne Cox), Richard Jenkins (Ted Treffon), Brad Pitt (Chad Feldheimer).

2009
The Men Who Stare at Goats
Director Grant Heslov *Screenwriter* Peter Straughan, from a book by Jon Ronson *Director of Photography* Robert Elswit *Composer* Rolfe Kent *Film Editor* Tatiana S. Riegel *Producers* George Clooney, Grant Heslov and Paul Lister. With George Clooney (Lyn Cassady), Jeff Bridges (Bill Django), Ewan McGregor (Bob Wilton), Kevin Spacey (Larry Hooper), Robert Patrick (Todd Nixon), Stephen Lang (Brigadier General Dean Hopgood).

Fantastic Mr. Fox
Director Wes Anderson *Screenwriters* Wes Anderson and Noah Baumbach, from a novel by Roald Dahl *Director of Photography* Tristan Oliver *Composer* Alexandre Desplat *Film Editors* Ralph Foster and Stephen Perkins *Producers* Allison Abbate, Wes Anderson, Jeremy Dawson and Scott Rudin. With the voices of George Clooney (Mr. Fox), Meryl Streep (Mrs. Fox), Jason Schwartzman (Ash), Wallace Wolodarsky (Kylie), Eric Chase Anderson (Kristofferson), Bill Murray (Badger), Michael Gambon (Franklin Bean).

Up in the Air
Director Jason Reitman *Screenwriters* Jason Reitman and Sheldon Turner, from a novel by Walter Kirn *Director of Photography* Eric Steelberg *Set Decorator* Linda Lee Sutton *Composer* Rolfe Kent *Film Editor* Dana E. Glauberman *Producers* Jeffrey Clifford, Daniel Dubiecki, Ivan Reitman and Jason Reitman. With George Clooney (Ryan Bingham), Vera Farmiga (Alex Goran), Anna Kendrick (Natalie Keener), Jason Bateman (Craig Gregory), Danny McBride (Jim Miller), Melanie Lynskey (Julie Bingham), Amy Morton (Kara Bingham), Sam Elliott (Maynard Finch).

2010
The American
Director Anton Corbijn *Screenwriter* Rowan Joffe, from a novel by Martin Booth *Director of Photography* Martin Ruhe *Set Decorator* Michelle Day *Composer* Herbert Grönemeyer *Film Editor* Andrew Hulme *Producers* Anne Carey, George Clooney, Jill Green, Grant Heslov and Ann Wingate. With George Clooney (Jack/Edward), Violante Placido (Clara), Irina Björklund (Ingrid), Thekla Reuten (Mathilde), Johan Leysen (Pavel), Paolo Bonacelli (Father Benedetto).

2011
The Ides of March
Director George Clooney *Screenwriters* George Clooney, Grant Heslov and Beau Willimon, from his play *Director of Photography* Phedon Papamichael *Set Decorator* Maggie Martin *Composer* Alexandre Desplat *Film Editor* Stephen Mirrione *Producers* George Clooney, Grant Heslov and Brian Oliver. With George Clooney (Governor Mike Morris), Ryan Gosling (Stephen Meyers), Philip Seymour Hoffman (Paul Zara), Paul Giamatti (Tom Duffy), Evan Rachel Wood (Molly Stearns), Marisa Tomei (Ida Horowicz), Jeffrey Wright (Senator Thompson).

The Descendants
Director Alexander Payne *Screenwriters* Alexander Payne, Nat Faxon and Jim Rash, from a novel by Kaui Hart Hemmings *Director of Photography* Phedon Papamichael *Set Decorator* Matt Callahan *Film Editor* Kevin Tent *Producers* Jim Burke, Alexander Payne and Jim Taylor. With George Clooney (Matt King), Shailene Woodley (Alexandra King), Amara Miller (Scottie King), Nick Krause (Sid), Patricia Hastie (Elizabeth King), Beau Bridges (Cousin Hugh), Robert Forster (Scott Thorson), Matthew Lillard (Brian Speer), Judy Greer (Julie Speer).

Touch of Evil (short film for The New York Times Magazine)
Director Alex Prager *Director of Photography* Ross Richardson *Composer* Ali Helnwein *Film Editor* Jonathan Schwartz *Producers* Arem Duplessis, Joanna Milter and Kathy Ryan.

With George Clooney, Jessica Chastain, Glenn Close, Viola Davis, Jean Dujardin, Kirsten Dunst, Ryan Gosling, Rooney Mara, Adepero Oduye, Gary Oldman, Brad Pitt, Michael Shannon, Mia Wasikowska.

2012
8 (video)
Director Rob Reiner *Screenwriter* Dustin Lance Black *Producer* Bruce Cohen. With George Clooney (David Boies), Martin Sheen (Theodore B. Olson), Brad Pitt (Chief Judge Vaughn R. Walker), Jamie Lee Curtis (Sandy Stier), Kevin Bacon (Charles Cooper).

2013
Gravity
Director Alfonso Cuarón *Screenwriters* Alfonso Cuarón, Jonás Cuarón and George Clooney (uncredited script collaborator) *Director of Photography* Emmanuel Lubezki *Set Decorators* Rosie Goodwin and Joanne Woollard *Composer* Steven Price *Film Editors* Alfonso Cuarón and Mark Sanger *Producers* Alfonso Cuarón and David Heyman. With George Clooney (Matt Kowalski), Sandra Bullock (Ryan Stone).

2014
The Monuments Men
Director George Clooney *Screenwriters* George Clooney and Grant Heslov, from a book by Robert M. Edsel and Bret Witter *Director of Photography* Phedon Papamichael *Set Decorator* Bernhard Henrich *Composer* Alexandre Desplat *Film Editor* Stephen Mirrione *Producers* George Clooney and Grant Heslov. With George Clooney (Frank Stokes), Matt Damon (James Granger), Bill Murray (Richard Campbell), Cate Blanchett (Claire Simone), John Goodman (Walter Garfield), Jean Dujardin (Jean-Claude Clermont).

2015
Tomorrowland
Director Brad Bird *Screenwriters* Damon Lindelof and Brad Bird, from a story by Damon Lindelof, Brad Bird and Jeff Jensen *Director of Photography* Claudio Miranda *Composer* Michael Giacchino *Film Editors* Walter Murch and Craig Wood *Producers* Brad Bird, Jeffrey Chernov and Damon Lindelof. With George Clooney (Frank Walker), Britt Robertson (Casey Newton), Judy Greer (Mom), Hugh Laurie (David Nix), Kathryn Hahn (Ursula).

Articles

Sam Alipour, 'Talking football and cinema with George Clooney', ESPN Page 2 (4 April 2008).

Anon., 'George Clooney and Stephen Gaghan on *Syriana*', Film4 (November 2005).

George Clooney, 'Hello reddit, George Clooney here. AMAA', www.reddit.com (28 January 2014).

Paul Fischer, 'Interview: George Clooney for "O Brother, Where Art Thou?"', www.darkhorizons.com (22 December 2000).

Mike Fleming, Jr, 'Hollywood Cowardice: George Clooney Explains Why Sony Stood Alone In North Korean Cyberterror Attack', www.deadline.com (18 December 2014).

Cal Fussman, 'George Clooney: What I've Learned', *Esquire* (13 December 2011).

A.J. Jacobs, 'The 9:10 to Crazyland', *Esquire* (17 March 2008).

Eric Kohn, 'Alexander Payne On "The Descendants" And Why It's a Minor Work', www.indiewire.com (24 October 2011).

Norman Lear, 'George Clooney', *Interview* (October 2005).

Adam Markovitz, 'George Clooney talks "The Monuments Men"', *Entertainment Weekly* (12 August 2013).

Chris Nashawaty, 'The Last Great Movie Star', *Look* (December 2005).

Alex Perry, 'Q&A with George Clooney: Hollywood Legend Talks Sudan, Satellites and How to Stop Atrocities', *Time* (27 April 2012).

Jonathan Romney, 'Double Vision', *The Guardian* (19 May 2000).

Robert Siegel, 'George Clooney on Acting, Fame, and Putting Down Your Cellphone Camera', *All Things Considered*, NPR (10 February 2012).

Books

Shana Cushman, *George Clooney: The Illustrated Biography*, Carlton Publishing Group, London, 2008.

Anthony Kaufman (ed.), *Steven Soderbergh: Interviews*, University Press of Mississippi, Jackson MS, 2002.

Kimberly Potts, *George Clooney: The Last Great Movie Star*, Applause Books, Milwaukee WI, 2011.

Clooney in *Welcome to Collinwood* (2002) by Anthony and Joe Russo.

Notes

1 'Faces Of Beauty: Yesterday & Today', AAFPRS Media Kit (15 January 2003).
2 Ibid.
3 Ibid.
4 Bernard Weinraub, 'George Clooney: The Playboy Interview', Playboy (July 2000).
5 Siobhan Synnot, 'There's something about George', Herald Sun (25 February 2012).
6 Pat Gallagher, 'Nick Clooney: Anchorman, Television Host, Print Journalist, Activist and, Oh, Yes, Father of George', Huffington Post (16 August 2013).
7 Bernard Weinraub, op. cit.
8 Pat Gallagher, op. cit.
9 Bernard Weinraub, op. cit.
10 Alex Bilmes, 'George Clooney: The Full Interview', Esquire (4 January 2014).
11 Bernard Weinraub, op. cit.
12 Ibid.
13 Robert Siegel, 'George Clooney on Acting, Fame, And Putting Down Your Cellphone Camera', All Things Considered, NPR (10 February 2012).
14 Bernard Weinraub, op. cit.
15 Alex Bilmes, op. cit.
16 Pauline Kael, 'The Man from Dream City', The New Yorker (14 July 1975).
17 Bernard Weinraub, op. cit.
18 Todd McCarthy,

'Review: From Dusk Till Dawn', Variety (21 January 1996).
19 Roger Ebert, 'Review: One Fine Day', Chicago Sun-Times (20 December 1996).
20 Janet Maslin, 'Enough Blood to Feed The Thirstiest Vampires', The New York Times (19 January 1996).
21 David Gergen, 'George Clooney on Fame, Pulling Pranks, and His Aunt Rosemary Clooney', Parade (22 September 2011).
22 Alex Bilmes, op. cit.
23 Jeremy Smith, Interview with Steven Soderbergh (19 November 2014).
24 Ibid.
25 Ibid.
26 Jennifer Vineyard, 'The Vulture Transcript: Steven Soderbergh on Haywire, Pranking Matt Damon, and His Looming Sabbatical', www.vulture.com (13 January 2012).
27 Jeremy Smith, 'Steven Soderbergh Talks Contagion And Much, Much More With Mr. Beaks', www.aintitcool.com (8 September 2011).
28 Stephen Schaefer, 'With Out of Sight, the Director of Sex, Lies, and Videotape Lends His Unique Vision to the Summer Blockbuster Wars', Boston Herald (23 June 1998).
29 Ibid.
30 Ibid.
31 Jeremy Smith, 2014, op. cit.

32 Ibid.
33 Roger Ebert, 'Review: Out of Sight', Chicago Sun-Times (19 June 1998).
34 Michael Fleming, 'George Clooney: The Mind Behind The Eyes', Movieline (1 October 2000).
35 Sharon Waxman, Rebels on the Backlot: Six Maverick Directors and How They Conquered the Hollywood System, HarperCollins (2005), p. 229.
36 Bernard Weinraub, op. cit.
37 Sharon Waxman, op. cit., p. 228.
38 Ibid., p. 229.
39 Three Kings, DVD Commentary, Warner Bros., 1999.
40 Jeremy Smith, 2014, op. cit.
41 Sharon Waxman, op. cit., p. 230.
42 A physical production executive oversees the studio's resources. They keep a watchful eye on budget and schedule.
43 Hearts of Darkness is a 1991 documentary about the making of Francis Ford Coppola's Apocalypse Now (1979).
44 Three Kings, DVD Commentary, op. cit.
45 Ibid.
46 Sharon Waxman, op. cit., p. 244.
47 Bernard Weinraub, op. cit.
48 Ned Zeman, 'The Admirable Clooney', Vanity Fair (October 2003).

49 Kevin Polowy, 'Role Recall: Mark Wahlberg on Boogie Nights, Three Kings and More', Yahoo! Movies (27 June 2014).
50 Stephen Galloway, 'George Clooney: The Private Life of a Superstar', The Hollywood Reporter (15 February 2012).
51 Michael Fleming, op. cit.
52 Daniel Fierman, 'Fun with George and Brad', Entertainment Weekly (8 June 2007).
53 Rebecca Ascher-Walsh and Steve Daly, 'Dark Days At Cannes', Entertainment Weekly (2 June 2000).
54 Disney (a.k.a. Touchstone Pictures) distributed the film in the United States.
55 James Lipton, Inside the Actors Studio – George Clooney, Bravo (31 January 2012).
56 Mariella Frostrup, 'Bedside manner', The Guardian (20 January 2002).
57 James Lipton, op. cit.
58 OK! UK, January 2001.
59 Noah Wyle, 'Buds', US Weekly (22 January 2001).
60 James Lipton, op. cit.
61 Mariella Frostrup, op. cit.
62 A.O. Scott, 'Film Review; Hail, Ulysses, Escaped Convict', The New York Times (22 December 2000).
63 Paul Karon, 'Clooney tunes prod'n pipeline', Variety (19 August 1997).

64 Michael Fleming, *op. cit.*

65 *Ibid.*

66 Mariella Frostrup, *op. cit.*

67 Michael Fleming, *op. cit.*

68 Bill O'Reilly is a conservative political commentator for Fox News who has clashed publicly with Clooney on several occasions.

69 Jeremy Smith, 2014, *op. cit.*

70 *Ibid.*

71 *Ibid.*

72 Stephanie Zacharek, 'Ocean's Eleven', *Salon* (7 December 2001).

73 Elvis Mitchell, 'For the New Rat Pack, It's a Ring-a-Ding Thing', *The New York Times* (7 December 2001).

74 Nev Pierce, 'Steven Soderbergh – Solaris', BBC Films (24 February 2003).

75 Berge Garabedian, 'Interview: J. Cameron', www.joblo.com (25 November 2002).

76 Jeremy Smith, 2014, *op. cit.*

77 *Ibid.*

78 Hugh Hart, 'Partners In Angst', *Sun Sentinel* (24 November 2002).

79 Geoff Andrew, 'Again, with 20% more existential grief', *The Guardian* (13 February 2003).

80 *Ibid.*

81 *Ibid.*

82 *Ibid.*

83 *Ibid.*

84 Jeremy Smith, 2014, *op. cit.*

85 *Ibid.*

86 *Ibid.*

87 Nev Pierce, 'Natascha McElhone – Solaris', BBC Films (10 February 2003).

88 Jeremy Smith, 2014, *op. cit.*

89 *Ibid.*

90 Nev Pierce, 'George Clooney – Solaris', BBC Films (10 February 2003).

91 Jeremy Smith, 2014, *op. cit.*

92 Owen Gleiberman, 'Review: Solaris', *Entertainment Weekly* (27 November 2002).

93 Todd McCarthy, 'Review: Solaris', *Variety* (20 November 2002).

94 Roger Ebert, 'Solaris', *Chicago Sun-Times* (22 November 2002).

95 Jeremy Smith, 2014, *op. cit.*

96 *Ibid.*

97 Caspar Milquetoast is a character created by H.T. Webster in the 1920s for his comic strip *The Timid Soul*. He became so popular that the term 'milquetoast' came into general American English usage to describe a timid, easily dominated person. (Gaghan seems to have inadvertently changed his first name.)

98 Drew McWeeny, 'Moriarty Interviews Stephen Gaghan About Syriana', www.aintitcool.com (17 November 2005).

99 Gavin Edwards, 'George Clooney: Renegade of the Year', *Rolling Stone* (15 December 2005).

100 Kapil Amarnath, 'Interview: Talking With George Clooney', *The Tech* (13 December 2005).

101 Gina McIntyre, 'George Clooney, Actor', *The Hollywood Reporter* (13 October 2006).

102 Kapil Amarnath, *op. cit.*

103 Miriam Zendle, 'Director Lee criticises Clooney Oscar speech', *Digital Spy* (21 March 2006).

104 Lina Lofaro, 'Q&A: George Clooney', *Time* (11 January 2008).

105 Jeremy Smith, 2014, *op. cit.*

106 Lina Lofaro, *op. cit.*

107 Tom Keogh, 'Director Interview: Tony Gilroy, "Michael Clayton"', *The Seattle Times* (7 October 2007).

108 Section Eight had officially closed down, but two films still remained for release: *Michael Clayton* and *The Informant!* (2009).

109 Lina Lofaro, *op. cit.*

110 Tom Keogh, *op. cit.*

111 Lina Lofaro, *op. cit.*

112 Ty Burr, 'Clooney makes a case for "Clayton"', *The Boston Globe* (5 October 2007).

113 Roger Ebert, 'Michael Clayton', *Chicago Sun-Times* (4 October 2007).

114 Ian Parker, 'Somebody Has To Be In Control', *The New Yorker* (14 April 2008).

115 Josh Spero, 'George Clooney should stick to being suave', *The Guardian* (4 October 2007).

116 *Ibid.*

117 Jeremy Smith, 2014, *op. cit.*

118 Drew McWeeny, 'Having The Moment: George Clooney', www.hitfix.com (12 September 2009).

119 Stephen Saito, 'Jason Reitman at the New Beverly', IFC (16 February 2010).

120 Anne Thompson, '20 Questions for Up in the Air's Jason Reitman', www.indiewire.com (29 November 2009).

121 John Hiscock, 'George Clooney interview', *The Telegraph* (16 October 2009).

122 Anne Thompson, *op. cit.*

123 John Hiscock, *op. cit.*

124 *Ibid.*

125 Kenneth Turan, 'Up in the Air', *Los Angeles Times* (4 December 2009).

126 Owen Gleiberman, 'Up in the Air', *Entertainment Weekly* (30 December 2009).

127 Stephanie Zacharek, '"Up in the Air": Take the next flight', *Salon* (4 December 2009).

128 John Hiscock, *op. cit.*

129 Jeremy Smith, 2014, *op. cit.*

130 John Hiscock, *op. cit.*

131 Stuart Jeffries, 'Anton Corbijn: "I know just enough not to look stupid"', *The Guardian* (25 November 2010).

132 Michael Slenske, 'Anton Corbijn is Still in Control', *Interview Magazine* (5 November 2010).

133 Stuart Jeffries, *op. cit.*

134 Rob Carnevale, 'The American – Anton Corbijn interview', www.indielondon.co.uk (November 2010).

135 *Ibid.*

136 Scott Macaulay, 'Dressing George Clooney: Costume Designer Suttirat Anne Larlarb on *The American*', *Focus Features* (17 August 2010).

137 Rob Carnevale, *op. cit.*

138 Roger Ebert, 'The American', *Chicago Sun-Times* (31 August 2010).

139 A.O. Scott, 'Traveling Man With Few Words and a Big Gun', *The New York Times* (31 August 2010).

140 Robert Koehler, 'Review: "The American"', *Variety* (31 August 2010).

141 Stuart Jeffries, *op. cit.*

142 Stephen Galloway, *op. cit.*

143 John Kiesewetter, 'George Clooney tapped Cincinnati roots to make "Ides of March"', *The Cincinnati Enquirer* (2 October 2011).

144 *Ibid.*

145 Nick Pinkerton, 'NYFF: Life is (Alexander) Payne', *The Village Voice* (28 September 2011).

146 Dave Davies, 'In Payne's "Descendants," Trouble In The Tropics', WBUR (17 November 2011).

147 John Hiscock, 'George

Clooney *The Descendants* interview: Is that an Oscar on the horizon?, *The Telegraph* (24 January 2012).

148 Scott Tobias, 'Alexander Payne', *A.V. Club* (15 November 2011).

149 *Ibid.*

150 Stephen Galloway, *op. cit.*

151 Sarah Wexler, 'Shailene Woodley on *The Descendants*, Crying Underwater, and George Clooney's Fart Machine', www.vulture.com (16 November 2011).

152 John Hiscock, 2012, *op. cit.*

153 Todd McCarthy, 'The Descendants: Telluride Film Review', *The Hollywood Reporter* (2 September 2011).

154 Ann Hornaday, 'The Descendants: Editorial Review', *The Washington Post* (18 November 2011).

155 Dana Stevens, 'The Descendants', *Slate* (17 November 2011).

156 John Hiscock, 2012, *op. cit.*

157 Marlow Stern, 'George Clooney's Powerful Golden Globes Speech on His Love For Amal and Je Suis Charlie', *The Daily Beast* (11 January 2015).

158 Jeremy Smith, 2014, *op. cit.*

159 Rebecca Ford, 'George Clooney to Direct Phone-Hacking Scandal Movie for Sony', *The Hollywood Reporter* (3 September 2014).

160 Jeremy Smith, 2014, *op. cit.*

Sidebar Notes

a Chris Jones, 'It's More Fun to Be the Painter Than the Paint', *Esquire* (December 2006).

b Mariella Frostrup, *op. cit.*

c Joe Morgenstern,

d 'Review: *Batman & Robin*', *The Wall Street Journal* (20 June 1997).

e Bernard Weinraub, *op. cit.*

f Alex Bilmes, *op. cit.*

Hilary de Vries, 'Capturing Cold War Fears, Live and in Black and White', *The New York Times* (9 April 2000).

g Reed Tucker, 'First Degree "Burn"', *New York Post* (7 September 2008).

h *Ibid.*

i Naomi Serviss, 'George Clooney, You're No Cary Grant', *The Wrap* (25 August 2009).

j Roxanna Bina, 'George Clooney is NOT Michael Clayton', *Independent Film Quarterly* (September 2006).

k Jeremy Smith, 2014, *op. cit.*

l Laura M. Holson, 'Trying to Combine Art and Box Office in Hollywood', *The New York Times* (17 January 2005).

m Jeremy Smith, 2014, *op. cit.*

n Gina McIntyre, *op. cit.*

o Wendy Boswell, 'Interview with *Ocean's Thirteen* stars Brad Pitt and George Clooney', www.crushable.com (9 June 2007).

p Rebecca Murray and Fred Topel, 'George Clooney Talks About "Confessions of a Dangerous Mind"', www.movies.about.com (December 2002).

q Rebecca Murray and Fred Topel, 'Drew Barrymore Talks About "Confessions of a Dangerous Mind"', www.movies.about.com (December 2002).

r Steven Kotler, 'George Clooney Q&A', *Variety* (8 January 2006).

s James Rocchi, 'Interview: David Strathairn of

Good Night, and Good Luck', www.moviefone.com (17 December 2005).

t Jeremy Smith, 2014, *op. cit.*

u *Ibid.*

v Dennis Lim, 'A Heartthrob Finds His Tough-Guy Side', *The New York Times* (14 September 2011).

w John Kiesewetter, *op. cit.*

x John Hiscock, 2012, *op. cit.*

y Rob Carnevale, 'Fantastic Mr. Fox – George Clooney interview', www.indielondon.co.uk (2009).

z *Ibid.*

aa Gina McIntyre, *op. cit.*

bb Dan P. Lee, 'Alfonso Cuarón Answers All Your Questions About *Gravity*', www.vulture.com (7 October 2013).

cc *Ibid.*

dd Sophia Savage, 'George Clooney on Fame, Failure & Success, Cuaron's "Gravity" and "Monuments Men"', www.indiewire.com (23 November 2012).

Clooney in Steven Soderbergh's *Ocean's Thirteen* (2007).

191

Original title:
George Clooney
© 2016 Cahiers du cinéma
SARL

Titre original :
George Clooney
© 2016 Cahiers du cinéma
SARL

This Edition published
by Phaidon Press Limited
under licence from Cahiers
du cinéma SARL,
18–20, rue Claude-Tillier,
75012 Paris, France
© 2016 Cahiers du cinéma
SARL.

Cette Édition est publiée par
Phaidon Press Limited avec
l'autorisation des Cahiers
du cinéma SARL,
18-20, rue Claude-Tillier,
75012 Paris, France
© 2016 Cahiers du cinéma
SARL.

Cahiers du cinéma
18–20, rue Claude-Tillier
75012 Paris

www.cahiersducinema.com

ISBN 978 0 7148 6806 6

A CIP catalogue record of this
book is available from the
British Library.

Editor:
Amélie Despérier-Bougdira
Project editor:
Céline Moulard
Series concept design:
Thomas Mayfried
Design: Pascale Coulon
Copy-editor: Lise Connellan
Proofreading: Anne McDowall
Picture research:
Carolina Lucibello
Reproduction: Ilc-Point 4

Printed in China

Acknowledgments

The author would like
to thank the following
people for their wisdom and
assistance, without which the
writing of this book would've
been impossible: Amélie
Desperier-Bougdira, Céline
Moulard, Steven Soderbergh,
Michael Sugar, Linda Smith,
Sarah Sprague and the
amazing Amy Nicholson.
And something more than
mere gratitude is due the
brilliant staff of the Margaret
Herrick Library in Beverly
Hills, California.